THE CHRISTIAN BUBBLE

Kyle Ferguson

© 2019 Kyle Ferguson All Rights Reserved

CONTENTS

Introduction 1
Sunday School 3
The Bible 6
The Devil 18
Voltaire 20
Thomas Paine 27
Robert Ingersoll 34
The Wright Brothers 37
Nikola Tesla 39
Swami Vivekananda 43
Bertrand Russell 45
Mother Teresa 47
    "Please tell Jesus to stop kissing me." 48
    "Mother was very concerned that we preserve our spirit of poverty." 51
    "Ask yourself what Jesus would do?" 53
    "I'm not a social worker. I do it for the church." 56
    "They are not true. They're all lies." 58
    "This miracle is a hoax." 65
    "Blind faith" 68

No One is Specially Chosen 72
A Strict Relationship 75
Bursting the Bubble.. 77
What Should I Believe? What Should I Do?... 79
Acknowledgments 82

INTRODUCTION

I have seen horrific injustice…and I have looked the other way.

In Baguio, Philippines, stands one of the most beautiful and luxurious churches I have ever seen. I gazed up at its lofty arches, knowing it is a proclamation to the world that God is love.

I looked down the steps of the cathedral and I saw orphan children who lived on the streets, wearing filthy clothes, without shoes, with unhappy faces, selling flowers.

I looked away.

It was awful to see such sad children, with no one to love them, holding flowers in their tiny hands, with no parents in sight.

What would you do?

Then I looked at the nearby rooftops and saw dogs chained on the tops of houses, surrounded by barbed wire, in direct sunlight, with no food or water, in tropical temperatures. Near the church there were more dogs, suffering in small cages.

It was too painful. I had to look away.

But I also looked away because I was taught to believe that the Church was doing God's work, and I feared going to Hell for eternity for questioning such divine authority.

I did not *want* to see.

What would you have done?

Three years later, back in Canada, I finally saw.

At the Eaton Centre in Toronto one day, as I was walking through the mall, I saw a man wearing a Canada Goose jacket.[1]

I approached him to ask if he knew about the cruelty involved in the making of his jacket. I explained that Canada Goose does not treat animals humanely. Coyotes are known to chew off their paws in a state of panic, their only means to free themselves from powerful and painful leg-hold traps.

As I told him of the horrific, unnecessary cruelty involved in making the jacket, he said, "I'm a devout Catholic, so I believe that human beings were put on the earth to dominate over creatures."

I told him that was indoctrination, and he agreed.

I knew he was living inside a bubble… just as I realized that I too had been living inside a bubble.

I was born and raised a Christian, and now I was questioning God.

The story you are about to read lead me to changing my perspective completely and becoming a human and animal rights activist, and co-founding The Light Movement, with my great friend Chris McGinn.[2]

I challenge you to read it through to the end.

---

[1] Kyle Ferguson. (2016, November) Retrieved from https://www.facebook.com/GoVegan182/videos/10154759669918610

[2] The Light Movement. (2019). Retrieved from https://www.facebook.com/lightmoveme

SUNDAY SCHOOL

I was chosen by God to be born into this world.

That is what my Sunday school teachers told me. They also told me that God, who lives in the sky, chose my parents.

I deduced that also meant that God chose poor children to be born into poverty.

I remembered seeing public service announcements on TV of starving children. I wondered why God selected me to be born into comfort and happiness while millions of others suffered.

My Sunday school teachers said that Jesus was the Son of God and that we must believe in him. I was taught that no one could go to Heaven without believing in Jesus Christ.

I asked my Sunday school teacher, "What about the children who are born into poverty? Do they go to Heaven?"

She replied, "They only go to Heaven if they believe in Jesus."

I thought this was wrong.

Not only was it unfair for a child to be born into poverty; many impoverished children have never had the chance to learn about—or believe in—Jesus.

It scared me to think that God would allow individuals to be punished for never having the opportunity to learn about Christianity. But I agreed to believe, because it was much worse than the alternative: to spend eternity in hell getting pitchforked by the Devil.

One day after Sunday school, I went inside the church where my parents were listening to the sermon. I sat down beside my father and noticed a man standing in the back of the room. He took money out of his pocket and placed it on top of an expensive-looking plate.

As the next hymn began, he walked down the aisles and passed the expensive-looking plate along to the parishioners.

I was in disbelief as the plate reached my father, who placed a five-dollar bill on top of it.

I wondered why the Church was asking its flock for money when it could ask God or Jesus instead.

I told my parents of my concerns and opinions about attending church and they began to listen.

My family and I went to church less and less, finally going only once a year, on Christmas Eve. But I stayed inside the bubble. I still believed the Church was connected to God, and that I would go to Heaven no matter what…as long as I believed in Jesus Christ.

In 2011, when I was living in the Philippines, I saw orphans being trafficked to sell flowers on the steps of beautiful churches, as dogs were held prisoner in filthy cages surrounded by sharp barbed wire fences.

I believed such terrible poverty and suffering did not apply to me, so why should I care?

And then, in 2016, a man in a trendy, fur-trimmed Canada Goose jacket said something that forced me to care.

Now I needed to know why any God would beseech orphan children to sell flowers outside of elaborate, lofty churches…or allow dogs to be imprisoned on top of houses surrounded by sharp barbed wire fences.

Why would God punish certain people and animals by having them born into such horrific circumstances?

Why was He not helping them?

Why was the Church spending so much money on building such ornate places of worship?

Why was it not helping those in desperate need?

My intuition told me that something was wrong.

THE BIBLE

I turned to the Bible for answers. What were these people getting wrong? I began by investigating the Old Testament. The man in the Canada Goose jacket said, "I'm a devout Catholic, so I believe that human beings were put on the earth to dominate over creatures."

Did the Bible really teach this?

I soon discovered that it did—in the very first chapter. In Genesis 1:26, I read, "Then God said, "Let Us make man in Our image, according to Our likeness. They will rule the fish of the sea, the birds of the sky, the livestock, all the earth, and the creatures that crawl on the earth."[3]

This did not seem to me like the teachings of a gentle Jesus. Dominating vulnerable species just because the Bible says we can? How is this not immoral?

According to Old Testament scholar Terence Fretheim,[4] the Hebrew verb translated as "have dominion" (rada) "must be understood in terms of caregiving, even nurturing, not exploitation."[5]

---

[3] All Bible quotes are from the *Holman Christian Standard Bible*, Christian Standard Bible®, Copyright © 2017 by Holman Bible Publishers. Used by permission. Christian Standard Bible® and CSB® are federally registered trademarks of Holman Bible Publishers. [ONLINE] Available at: https://www.biblestudytools.com/csb/

[4] Terence E. Fretheim. (2018, January 26). Retrieved from https://en.wikipedia.org/w/index.php?title=Terence_E._Fretheim&oldid=822539155

[5] Pregeant, R. (2016). *For the Healing of the Nation: A Biblical Vision*. Eugene, OR: Cascade Books. p. 175.

But this is Fretheim's interpretation. Many other people whom I have spoken to, including the devout Catholic wearing a CG jacket, see this biblical verse as domination over non-human species.

I read on.

In Genesis 2:15–18, it says,

> The Lord God took the man and placed him in the garden of Eden to work it and watch over it.
>
> And the Lord God commanded the man, "You are free to eat from any tree of the garden, but you must not eat from the tree of the knowledge of good and evil, for on the day you eat from it, you will certainly die."
>
> Then the Lord God said, "It is not good for the man to be alone. I will make a helper who is like him."

And from Adam's rib, it says, God created Eve.

The Bible obviously is not a reliable reproductive anatomy lesson. Can it be a reliable lesson in morals? It does not start with love. It starts with a threat: The Lord God tells Adam that he will die if he eats from the tree of knowledge of good and evil. How can you know what is moral if you are forbidden to learn about good and evil?

From the beginning, the basis of Christianity gives us not love, not knowledge, but fear.

What did Adam and Eve do? They ate the fruit, made God angry, and blamed an animal for it. This is what Genesis 3:1–5 tells us:

> Now the serpent was the most cunning of all the wild animals that the Lord God had made. He said to the woman, "Did God really say, 'You can't eat from any tree in the garden'?" The woman said to the serpent, "We may eat the fruit from the trees in the garden. But about the fruit of the tree in the middle of the garden, God said, 'You must not eat it or touch

> it, or you will die.'" "No! You will not die," the serpent said to the woman. "In fact, God knows that when you eat it your eyes will be opened and you will be like God, knowing good and evil."
>
> Then the woman saw that the tree was good for food and delightful to look at, and that it was desirable for obtaining wisdom. So she took some of its fruit and ate [it]; she also gave [some] to her husband, [who was] with her, and he ate [it].

Adam and Eve wanted to know what was wrong and what was right; they did not just want to take the Lord's word for it. So they disobeyed, and made God angry, and blamed a talking snake, as if there had ever been such a thing.

But let's say the talking snake existed and it wanted Adam and Eve to know truth and own their own minds. Why is that bad? And then I realized that God wanted this situation to happen. He created the talking snake, like he created everything, according to the story. He wanted it to induce Adam and Eve into sinning so he could punish them.

He found out, of course. He always knew. And He punished them. Genesis 3:8–16:

> Then the man and his wife heard the sound of the Lord God walking in the garden at the time of the evening breeze, and they hid themselves from the Lord God among the trees of the garden.
>
> So the Lord God called out to the man and said to him, "Where are you?"
>
> And he said, "I heard You in the garden, and I was afraid because I was naked, so I hid."
>
> Then He asked, "Who told you that you were naked? Did you eat from the tree that I had commanded you not to eat from?" Then the man replied, "The woman You gave to be

> with me—she gave me [some fruit] from the tree, and I ate." So the Lord God asked the woman,
>
> "What is this you have done?" And the woman said, "It was the serpent. He deceived me, and I ate."
>
> Then the Lord God said to the serpent: "Because you have done this, you are cursed more than any livestock and more than any wild animal. You will move on your belly and eat dust all the days of your life. I will put hostility between you and the woman, and between your seed and her seed."
>
> He said to the woman: "I will intensify your labor pains; you will bear children in anguish. Your desire will be for your husband, yet he will dominate you."

The story of Adam and Eve teaches us that God punishes us for our mistakes—our sins—and it teaches us that we have all been born sinners because of what our distant ancestors did. It teaches us that God made us so he could punish us.

It puts fear into our hearts and minds.

As long as woman regards the Bible as the charter of her rights, she will be the slave of man. The Bible was not written by a woman. Inside its covers there is only embarrassment and disgrace for her. She is seen as the property of man. She is as much beneath her husband as her husband is beneath Christ.

The Bible dictates this in Ephesians 5:22–24:

> Wives, submit to your own husbands as to the Lord, for the husband is head of the wife as also Christ is head of the church. He is the Savior of the body. Now as the church submits to Christ, so wives should [submit] to their husbands in everything.

This does not sound like a loving God. It sounds like a dictator who is sexist. The mistreatment of women in the Bible does not stop there. Read Deuteronomy 22:28–29:

> If a man encounters a young woman, a virgin who is not engaged, takes hold of her and rapes her, and they are discovered, the man who raped her must give the young woman's father 50 silver [shekels], and she must become his wife because he violated her. He cannot divorce her as long as he lives.

This is so horrible; few people would admit to believing such a thing today. But it's right there, in the manual for Christianity, the supposed "word of God": a story of a divine dictator who is cruel to men and even crueler to women.

The Bible makes it clear that selling your daughter into sexual slavery is acceptable. In Exodus 21:7–11, it says,

> When a man sells his daughter as a slave, she is not to leave as the male slaves do. If she is displeasing to her master, who chose her for himself, then he must let her be redeemed. He has no right to sell her to foreigners because he has acted treacherously toward her. Or if he chooses her for his son, he must deal with her according to the customary treatment of daughters. If he takes an additional wife, he must not reduce the food, clothing, or marital rights of the first wife. And if he does not do these three things for her, she may leave free of charge, without any exchange of money.

Do you think this is just something from the distant past?

Women are still being sold into sexual slavery to this day throughout the world. The International Labour Organization estimates that there are 4.8 million people trapped in forced sexual exploitation globally and 99 percent of the victims are women.[6]

The Bible is supposed to have been written by the Lord God and it

---

[6] Forced labour, modern slavery and human trafficking (Forced labour, modern slavery and human trafficking). (n.d.). Retrieved from https://www.ilo.org/global/topics/forced-labour/lang--en/index.htm

gives people justification to sell their daughters into sexual slavery.

The divine dictator is even crueler to animals. I already knew that they were to be ruled over by humans. This includes sacrifices, which are featured throughout the Bible. Then I got to the story of Noah.

According to Genesis 6:17–22, the Lord God told Noah that he was going to flood the earth because it had become corrupt with violence.

The Lord God then gave Noah instructions to build an ark (a big boat) to save himself, as well as his wife, sons, and his sons' wives from an all-encompassing flood. God would also save animals…but only two of each. All the rest were drowned mercilessly:

> "Understand that I am bringing a deluge—floodwaters on the earth to destroy all flesh under heaven with the breath of life in it. Everything on earth will die. But I will establish My covenant with you, and you will enter the ark with your sons, your wife, and your sons' wives. You are also to bring into the ark two of every living thing of all flesh, male and female, to keep them alive with you. Two of everything—from the birds according to their kinds, from the livestock according to their kinds, and from every animal that crawls on the ground according to its kind—will come to you so that you can keep them alive. Take with you every kind of food that is eaten; gather it as food for you and for them." And Noah did this. He did everything that God had commanded him.

Why is the Lord God allowing people to sin in the first place? Why does He have to "flood the earth" to annihilate those who may not have committed sin?

Why is the Lord God drowning innocent and vulnerable animals?

And then, in Genesis 8:20–21, I read what happened after the flood dried up and the ark landed:

> Then Noah built an altar to the Lord. He took some of every

kind of clean animal and every kind of clean bird and offered burnt offerings on the altar.

When the Lord smelled the pleasing aroma, He said to Himself, "I will never again curse the ground because of man, even though man's inclination is evil from his youth."

The Lord God appreciates animal sacrifice.

After I read this passage, Old Testament scholar Terence Fretheim's translation of God offering caregiving did not make sense.

Why would Noah sacrifice innocent animals to the Lord God after keeping them safe inside the ark for all of that time? After all, he was supposed to preserve two of every kind so that they could reproduce and multiply. Were they saved just to be killed?

Why is the Lord God claiming that "man's inclination is evil from his youth"? Are we, too, born only to be tortured and killed?

God, who is supposed to be the most powerful and influential figure, the great Father, is telling the reader that he or she is "evil from youth." What do we think of fathers who always tell their children that they're bad and must be punished? What do you think of a father who drowns innocent animals and is pleased by animal sacrifice?

Of course, we have no good reason to believe any of this. There were only eight people on the ark; how were they supposed to care for thousands of animals? There needed to be enough food for all of them...not for 40 days: that is just how long it rained. They were all in that ark for over 375 days before they finally opened the door and stepped out.[7]

For that matter, how were they supposed to have built the ark at all? As Bill Nye, the science guy, has pointed out, much larger crews of experienced shipbuilders have been unable to build wooden ships close

---

[7] Untitled. (n.d.). Retrieved from http://www.arkonararat.com/Timeline.html

to that size that would stay afloat.[8]

The whole story is preposterous. That is why we are supposed to believe it: just to show that we will take "God's word" on anything and everything, and never think and conclude for ourselves.

We are also supposed to take God's word that homosexuality is "an abomination." Leviticus 20:13 says, "If a man sleeps with a man as with a woman, they have both committed an abomination. They must be put to death; their blood is on their own hands."

They just want to love each other, and the Bible says they must be put to death. Men raping girls and parents selling their daughter into sexual slavery is okay with this despot God. But two men in love must die.

Christianity indoctrinated me to believe that homosexuality is a crime. Then I moved to the Philippines and met a lot of people who were homosexual. How could I listen to this tyrant God when there were wonderful people in front of me who just wanted to love, be loved, and live their life being happy?

This tyrant God is the God of the Old Testament. Many Christians say that in the New Testament Jesus changed everything, but the Old Testament is part of the Bible, and even Jesus said that these laws still apply. In Matthew 5:18, he said, "For I assure you: Until heaven and earth pass away, not the smallest letter or one stroke of a letter will pass from the law until all things are accomplished."

Jesus warned people strongly not to sin and told them they would go to Hell if they did—see Mark 9:43–49:

> And if your hand causes your downfall, cut it off. It is better for you to enter life maimed than to have two hands and go to hell—the unquenchable fire, [where Their worm does not

---

[8] Answers in Genesis. (2014, February 4). Bill Nye Debates Ken Ham - HD (Official). Retrieved from
https://www.youtube.com/watch?v=z6kgvhG3AkI&feature=youtu.be&t=4305

die, and the fire is not quenched.] And if your foot causes your downfall, cut it off. It is better for you to enter life lame than to have two feet and be thrown into hell— [the unquenchable fire, where Their worm does not die, and the fire is not quenched.] And if your eye causes your downfall, gouge it out. It is better for you to enter the kingdom of God with one eye than to have two eyes and be thrown into hell, where Their worm does not die, and the fire is not quenched. For everyone will be salted with fire.

The New Testament does not oppose slavery either. In Ephesians 6:5–7, the Apostle Paul wrote, "Slaves, obey your human masters with fear and trembling, in the sincerity of your heart, as to Christ. Don't [work only] while being watched, in order to please men, but as slaves of Christ, do God's will from your heart. Render service with a good attitude, as to the Lord and not to men." The Bible was used to justify slavery in the United States.[9]

Slavery hasn't gone away, either. There are still 40 million slaves in the world today. There are more slaves in the world today than there are people in the state of California, the largest state by population in the United States.[10]

What do you think about slavery?

And the Bible does not care about animals.

I read Ecclesiastes 3:21: "Who knows if the spirit of people rises upward and the spirit of animals goes downward to the earth?" Each time resurrection is mentioned in the Bible, it is in regard to a human being. Romans 5:12 says, "Therefore, just as sin entered the world through one man, and death through sin, in this way death spread to all men, because all sinned."

---

[9] Rae, N. (2018, February 23). How Christian Slaveholders Used the Bible to Justify Slavery. Retrieved from http://time.com/5171819/christianity-slavery-book-excerpt/

[10] Ending modern slavery. (n.d.). Retrieved from
https://www.thomsonreuters.com/en/reports/modern-slavery.html

In other words, Jesus died and rose again to remove the penalty of sin for humans, but not for animals. Except for that talking snake, animals are not punished for sin as non-believers are. But because animals have not sinned, they cannot be redeemed. Animals do not go to Hell *or* Heaven when they die. Your dog won't go to Heaven.

I thought this was unfair because animals are living sentient beings, and they never had the opportunity to read the Bible or become Christians. Why should they be punished and forbidden from entering Heaven?

They also had no choice to be born as a non-human animal. It was out of their control.

Just as it was out of our control. The Bible tells us that we must continue to be punished for mistakes that were completely outside of our control and were made before we were born: the sin of Adam. All of creation, which God made, was corrupted—Romans 8:22: "For we know that the whole creation has been groaning together with labor pains until now."

But Jesus also said some things about caring for others. He did some things, too, and his Church does not follow those examples.

In the Gospel of Matthew, 15:32–39, Jesus turns a few loaves of bread and a few fish into enough food to feed thousands of people.

> Now Jesus summoned His disciples and said, "I have compassion on the crowd, because they've already stayed with Me three days and have nothing to eat. I don't want to send them away hungry; otherwise they might collapse on the way." The disciples said to Him, "Where could we get enough bread in this desolate place to fill such a crowd?"
>
> "How many loaves do you have?" Jesus asked them. "Seven," they said, "and a few small fish."
>
> After commanding the crowd to sit down on the ground, He took the seven loaves and the fish, and He gave thanks, broke

them, and kept on giving them to the disciples, and the disciples [gave them] to the crowds. They all ate and were filled. Then they collected the leftover pieces-seven large baskets full. Now those who ate were 4,000 men, besides women and children. After dismissing the crowds, He got into the boat and went to the region of Magadan.

Currently in the world today, 795 million people in the world do not get the food they need to live a healthy life. [11]

Jesus had the ability to turn a small amount of bread into enough to feed thousands of people. Why are modern churches not using all their resources to feed the hundreds of millions of people who are starving today?

They are supposed to be agents of God and must be doing everything they can to help people.

In the Philippines, orphan children are living on the streets selling flowers. They are so poverty-stricken that they are unable to attend school. The rich churches there could afford to lift them out of poverty.

They do not. What is their excuse?

In Matthew 19:24, Jesus says, "Again I tell you, it is easier for a camel to go through the eye of a needle than for a rich person to enter the kingdom of God."

Did you ever know a wealthy person who unloaded their bank account because of that verse? Have you ever seen the Church set an example in following it?

According to the website *The Richest*, Christian religions including Protestantism, Televangelism, Episcopalianism, the Church of

---

[11] World Hunger Statistics. (n.d.). Retrieved from https://www.foodaidfoundation.org/world-hunger-statistics.html

England, the Church of Jesus Christ of Latter-Day Saints, and the Roman Catholic Church have tens of billions of dollars among them.[12]

Meanwhile, hundreds of millions of people are starving around the world, without access to clean water, food, shelter, or education.

But instead of helping people who are in desperate need, Christian religions preach that those born into horrific poverty are not the chosen ones.

Christian religions want people to live in fear and submit to it.

---

[12] Said, S. (2013, August 12). The 10 Richest Religions in the World | TheRichest. Retrieved from https://www.therichest.com/rich-list/world/the-10-richest-religions-in-the-world

THE DEVIL

The Church does not just teach us to fear God. It also teaches us to be afraid of the Devil. The Devil is a figure the Church uses to scare people. I was taught in Sunday school that if I did not believe in God and Jesus, I would go for eternity to Hell where the Devil lived.

But where did this Devil actually come from?

In Jeremy Rifkin's great book *Beyond Beef: The Rise and Fall of The Cattle Culture*, he describes how the belief of the Devil came to be.

Rifkin begins by comparing the Mithraic cult with Christianity. If emperor Constantine had not converted to Christianity, the Mithraic cult might have become the true religion of the western world. The Mithraic cult celebrated the birthdate of the sun on December 25. The Christian religion took the Mithraic holy day making December 25 Christ's birthday. The two cults also believed that those who believed in the faith would go to heaven and the non-believers would go to hell.[13]

Christianity took animal sacrifices from the Mithraic cult and substituted the blood of Christ for the blood of the bull, as Jack Randolph Conrad explains:

> Disciples of the Mithraic faith were baptized into the cult on special holy days. Worshipers lined up in a pit under a bull. The priest then reenacted the Mithraic myth, ending in the

---

[13] Rifkin, J. (1992). *Beyond Beef: The Rise and Fall of the Cattle Culture*. New York: Penguin Books. p. 22.

slaughter of the animal.... After being purified in holy blood, they were each given a small portion of seed from the bull's testicles to eat, ensuring their immortality on judgment day.[14]

This was changed to the fellowship, eating the "body and blood" of the sacrificed Jesus. Rifken clarifies how Christians transformed the Mithraic bull god into their new image of dimness, which turned into the Devil incarnate.[15]

The Devil came from torturing and killing animals and is now used in modern day Christianity to strike fear into the hearts of believers and prospective converts, to ensure they live in fear and obey the Church.

I had turned to the Bible to try to find reason and compassion. Instead I found superstition, fear, tyranny, oppression of woman, and rejection of reason and independent thought.

It showed me not just blind faith, but blinding faith.

Being forced to believe based on fear without evidence is psychological torture.

I was in shock and needed to turn somewhere else to find reason and compassion.

I turned to the undisputed leader of the Age of Enlightenment, a man who was against tyranny, bigotry, and cruelty, a man who advocated for animal rights. A man who was also against organized religion.

---

[14] Conrad, J.R. (1973), *The Horn and the Sword: The History of the Bull As Symbol of Power and Fertility*. Westport CT: Greenwood Press, p. 51.

[15] Rifkin, *Beyond Beef*, p. 23.

VOLTAIRE

Born in 1694, in Paris, France, Francois Marie Arouet was one of the greatest writers and philosophers in France's history. He was relentless, writing up to eighteen hours each day. He wrote plays, poems, essays, and more than 20,000 influential letters and over 2,000 books during his lifetime. He went by the pen name Voltaire.[16]

Voltaire was against organized religion at a time when France was run by a corrupt state church and strict censorship laws. He risked large penalties by breaking censorship laws and questioning religious and political thought. He believed the best way to break the corrupt church's power over people's hearts and minds was to question its divine authority.[17]

He wrote *Dictionnaire philosophique* [The Philosophical Dictionary], which criticized Christianity for superstition, intolerance, and irrational preachings without knowledge or reason.

Voltaire believed organized religion was based on human fictions and superstition. In *The Philosophical Dictionary*, he wrote:

> The superstitious man is to the rogue what the slave is to the tyrant. Further, the superstitious man is governed by the fanatic and becomes fanatic. Superstition born in Paganism,

---

[16] Andrews, E. (2014, November 21). 10 Things You Should Know About Voltaire. Retrieved from https://www.history.com/news/10-things-you-should-know-about-voltaire

[17] Wilson, R. (2016, October 28). Who Was Voltaire? Retrieved from https://www.youtube.com/watch?v=7m5GuFD0f9Q

adopted by Judaism, infested the Christian Church from the earliest times. All the fathers of the Church, without exception, believed in the power of magic. The Church always condemned magic, but she always believed in it: she did not excommunicate sorcerers as madmen who were mistaken, but as men who were really in communication with the devil.[18]

Where should we turn for truth?

It is better to trust in what we learn from nature than in what we learn from religion; I prefer to rely on natural law than on human fictions.[19]

Voltaire was also a human rights activist who stood up to monstrous injustice.

Voltaire wrote his *Treatise on Toleration* after he learned of the case of Jean Calas, a Protestant merchant from Toulouse who had been wrongly convicted of murdering his twenty-eight-year-old son.

Toulouse, like all of France, was Catholic, but it had Protestants in it as well. Every year, Catholics of Toulouse celebrated the anniversary of the massacre of Protestants, which took place on May 17, 1562. On that date, thousands of Protestants took cover in Toulouse, agreeing to give up their weapons in return for safekeeping. As soon as they gave up their weapons, the Catholics slaughtered them.[20]

1762 was the two hundredth anniversary of this event. It was also the year of Marc-Antoine Calas's death.

Marc-Antoine, Jean Calas's son, had obtained a degree in law, but did

---

[18] Voltaire. (2006). The Project Gutenberg eBook of Voltaire's Philosophical Dictionary. Produced by Sutherland, J. and Reigel, L. and the Online Distributed Proofreading Team. Retrieved from http://www.gutenberg.org/files/18569/18569-h/18569-h.htm

[19] Voltaire. (2016). *Treatise on Toleration*. London, England: Penguin UK. p. 60. Quote by Voltaire.

[20] Voltaire. (2016). *Treatise on Toleration*. p. 5, note 6.

not have a certificate of catholicity, and he refused to convert to the Catholic faith. French law restricted members of the Protestant faith from entering certain careers.

One day Marc-Antoine lost money gambling and decided he'd had enough. He told his friend, Gaubert Lavaisse, a nineteen-year-old visiting from Bordeaux who had arrived in Toulouse the previous evening, that he planned to commit suicide.

The night of Marc-Antoine's death, Jean Calas, his wife, Marc-Antoine (their eldest son), Pierre (their second son), and Gaubert Lavaisse ate dinner together. Immediately following dinner, Marc-Antoine disappeared, and everyone else retreated to a small lounge. Later that night, when Gaubert Lavaisse was leaving, he and Pierre Calas went downstairs and discovered Marc-Antoine hanging from a door near the cellar. They saw that his clothes were neatly folded on a table, his shirt had no wrinkles, his body had no scratches or bruises, and his hair was well groomed.

Lavaisse and Pierre, immediately ran for surgeons and the magistrate.[21]

While they were out, the family began crying aloud.

A mob of people heard their cries and gathered outside the house. Because they were superstitious, violent people who hated Protestants and because they knew the Calas family were Protestant, they accused Jean Calas, his wife, Pierre, Gaubert Lavaisse, and their devout Catholic housemaid, Jeanne Viguière, of murdering Marc-Antoine to prevent him from converting to the Catholic religion.

The accusations had no basis. Jean Calas was a compassionate man who had previously granted his third son, Louis, his request to convert to Catholicism.[22] Calas also employed Jeanne Viguière, a devout

---

[21] Voltaire, & McCabe, J. (1912). *A Treatise on Toleration and Other Essays*. New York and London: G.P. Putnam's Sons. p. 2.

[22] Voltaire, & McCabe, J. (1912). *A Treatise on Toleration and Other Essays*. p. 2.

Catholic, as his servant. She had looked after his children for thirty years.

That didn't matter. The combination of accusations from the people of Toulouse and the two hundredth anniversary of the massacre led the presiding magistrate of Toulouse, François-Raymond David de Beaudrigue, to act on impulse. He had the Calas family arrested and prosecuted without warrants.[23]

A group of thirteen judges met to decide the case despite the fact there was no evidence against Jean Calas or his family. When Marc-Antoine was found, his hair was combed, his clothes had no wrinkles, and he had no major cuts or bruises. Marc-Antoine was in his late twenties and he was a strong man. Jean Calas was sixty-four years old, and he had poor balance from his swollen and weak limbs.[24] How could this murder have been committed without any sign of a struggle?

Despite having no evidence against the family, on March 9, 1762, the judges voted eight to five in favor of executing Jean Calas on the wheel. The judges believed that Jean Calas was a frail old man and would confess to killing his son as he was tortured. First, he was taken to the torture chamber, where his limbs were bound to a bar and attached to an arrangement of pulley's. His body was stretched until his arms and legs were torn from their sockets, as the magistrate, François-Raymond David de Beaudrigue, interrogated him, but Calas refused to confess.[25]

Then Calas's mouth was held open with two short sticks and he was forced to swallow thirty pints of water. This caused his body to balloon, expanding to twice its normal size, yet Calas refused to confess to murdering his son. He was then taken outside and tied to a

---

[23] Armstrong, K. (2015, March 13). Broken on the Wheel. Retrieved from https://www.themarshallproject.org/2015/03/13/broken-on-the-wheel

[24] *A Treatise on Toleration and Other Essays.* p.8.

[25] Armstrong, K. Broken on the Wheel.

cross in the cathedral square and each of his limbs was shattered in two places by the executioner's iron bar.[26]

Calas did not confess.

Instead, he asked God to testify and declare his innocence while asking Him to pardon his judges. The executioner finished Calas by strangling him. His body was burned on a pyre.[27]

Jean Cala's perseverance and refusal to admit to any crime compelled the judges into giving a second sentence. They decided the mother, her son Pierre, Lavaisse, and the Catholic housemaid should all be set free. But one of the judges pointed out that their second decision countered their first one, due to the fact that the family were in each other's presence when the murder was supposed to have happened. The judges knew that if they released the family, it would declare that Jean Calas was innocent, and it would prove that they made a horrible mistake.[28]

The judges instead decided to send Pierre into exile without any resources as an act of "mercy." But before Pierre left Toulouse, and while he was still imprisoned, a Dominican entered his cell and threatened that he would be tortured and killed as his father was, if he did not convert to the Catholic faith, but Pierre refused.

Later when Pierre was leaving town, he met a priest who specialized in religious conversions. Pierre was forced by the priest to return to Toulouse. He was then locked in a Dominican convent and was forced to study the Catholic faith, until he finally escaped.[29]

---

[26] Goldstone, L., & Goldstone, N. (2003). *Out of the Flames: The Remarkable Story of a Fearless Scholar, a Fatal Heresy, and One of the Rarest Books in the World.* New York, NY: Broadway Books. p. 256.

[27] Armstrong, K. (2015, March 13). Broken on the Wheel.

[28] *A Treatise on Toleration and Other Essays.* p. 10.

[29] Voltaire, *Treatise on Toleration*, p. 11. Pierre Calas escaped and travelled to Geneva, on 4 July 1762 where Voltaire interviewed him.

Jean Calas's wife had seen that one of her sons had hanged himself. Her husband had been unjustly tortured and killed. Another son had been exiled and then locked up. Her daughters were seized and taken to a Catholic convent. Finally, she was stripped of all her possessions and left alone without food and without hope in the world.[30]

All of this happened because Marc-Antoine was Protestant and could not get into law because he could not produce a certificate of catholicity.

Voltaire was in his late sixties when he learned about this monstrous injustice. He became convinced and outraged that Calas had been wrongly convicted. Voltaire persuaded Jean Calas's wife to appeal the verdict. Then he focused on the superstitious and irrational behaviour of the Catholics in Toulouse who caused Jean Calas to be accused of murdering his own son and was broken on the wheel. Voltaire helped to write legal documents, worked with lawyers, and relentlessly used every resource he could for support. He also hired and sent a young merchant to Toulouse to further investigate the case.

His hard work built huge momentum, influencing the French government to reopen Calas's case in 1763. The following year, the French government dismissed Calas's conviction and ordered a new trial.

On March 9, 1765, three years after Jean Calas was indicted, a board of forty judges reported its consistent decision: Jean Calas was vindicated. Powerless to reestablish his life, the court reestablished his great name.

Voltaire's persistence and relentless hard work redeemed Jean Calas. The case became a foundation for religious toleration and human rights, and an argument against the death penalty.[31]

Voltaire helped me realize that religion is used to control people. As

---

[30] *A Treatise on Toleration and Other Essays*. p. 11.

[31] Armstrong, K. Broken on the Wheel.

the Roman philosopher Lucius Annaeus Seneca is often credited with saying, "Religion is regarded by the common people as true, by the wise as false, and by rulers as useful."[32]

Another person who realized this and supported the French Revolution was Thomas Paine.

---

[32] The quote may actually be a paraphrase of Edward Gibbon. See Talk: Seneca the Younger - Wikiquote. (n.d.). Retrieved February 17, 2019, from https://en.wikiquote.org/wiki/Talk:Seneca_the_Younger

THOMAS PAINE

My country is the world, and my religion is to do good.
—Thomas Paine, *The Rights of Man* [33]

Thomas Paine was an English-American political activist, philosopher, pamphleteer, and abolitionist who fought for justice and freedom. He was born in Thetford, England, in 1737 to a Quaker father and Anglican mother. Paine received little formal education growing up, but did learn to read, write, and perform arithmetic. At the age of thirteen, he began working with his father as a staymaker in Thetford, a shipbuilding town. He tried various occupations unsuccessfully before becoming an excise tax collecting officer.

In the summer of 1772, Paine published *The Case of the Officers of Excise* because the overworked and underpaid excisemen urged him to address Parliament on their behalf. He wrote to Parliament and was dismissed from the excise office.

Paine's situation seemed hopeless. To make matters worse, his wife, Mary Lambert, passed away during childbirth.[34]

Paine loved science and reading. He would spend a lot of his time in bookstores. He connected with brilliant people by attending lectures

---

[33] Text < Thomas Paine - The Rights of Man (1791-1792) < 1786-1800 < Documents < American History from Revolution to Reconstruction and beyond. (n.d.). Retrieved from http://www.let.rug.nl/usa/documents/1786-1800/thomas-paine-the-rights-of-man/text.php

[34] Foner, P. S. (n.d.). Thomas Paine | Biography, Common Sense, & Rights of Man. Retrieved from https://www.britannica.com/biography/Thomas-Paine

on scientific subjects. Paine met Benjamin Franklin in London after befriending a London astronomer. Franklin saw great potential in Paine. He advised Paine to move to America and gave him letters of introduction.

At the age of thirty-seven, Thomas Paine left England for America He arrived in Philadelphia on November 30, 1774. He rented a room at Market and Front streets, from which he could see the Philadelphia Slave Market.[35]

Paine was hired to edit the *Pennsylvania Magazine* for eighteen months.[36]

He published a minimum of seventeen articles, possibly as many as twenty-six. Each one was signed with pen names such as "Vox Populi" and "Justice, and Humanity."[37]

His first article against slavery, published on March 8, 1775, had a huge impact in denouncing slavery in America. Five days after the article was published, the American Anti-Slavery Society was formed in Philadelphia.[38]

His second article was against dueling; the third on the treatment of prisoners. Paine declared that prisoners should be rehabilitated, not punished and degraded in prison. Paine's fourth article was on the rights of women, the first ever published in the New World. His fifth was in favour of forming societies for the prevention of cruelty to children and animals.[39]

On January 10, 1776, Paine published *Common Sense*, a fifty-page

---

[35] Powell, J. (1996, January 1). Thomas Paine, Passionate Pamphleteer for Liberty | Jim Powell. Retrieved from https://fee.org/articles/thomas-paine-passionate-pamphleteer-for-liberty

[36] Foner, Thomas Paine.

[37] Powell, Thomas Paine, Passionate Pamphleteer for Liberty

[38] Ingersoll, R. G. (1900). *The Works of Robert G. Ingersoll, Vol. XI (in 12 Volumes)*. New York, The Dresden Publishing Company. p. 323.

[39] Ingersoll, R.G. *The Complete Works of Robert Ingersoll*, vol. IV, p. 42.

pamphlet everyone could understand and defend. It was filled with contention, reason, influence, and unanswerable rationale, criticizing the British government and arguing for America's separation from Britain. *Common Sense* helped lead to the Declaration of Independence on July 4, 1776.

Common Sense sold more than 500,000 copies in a short time, more than any other single publication at the time.

Paine was a great man who wanted justice and equality. He was a best-selling author, yet he lived in poverty, since he refused to accept profits from his book sales because he wanted his books to build momentum by being affordable and widely circulated.[40]

After publishing *Common Sense*, the pamphlet that helped lead to America's independence from Britain, Thomas Paine was on top of the world. He could have retired, but instead continued to do good and benefit mankind.

In May 1787, Paine traveled from America to France, and then to London (Sept. 1787), with the intention of meeting scientific leaders [41], to secure financing for an iron bridge that he had designed. [42] Paine planned to assemble the bridge over the Schuylkill River, close to Philadelphia, once he had secured funding for the bridge. But when Paine got to England, he quickly aborted his bridge-building plan after he learned that Prime Minister, William Pitt, was intending on including England in a war with France over Holland. In December 1789, Paine anonymously published a warning against the attempt of Pitt to involve England in a war with France over Holland. Paine reminded the British people that war had "But one thing certain and

---

[40] Foner, Thomas Paine.

[41] Paine, T., & Kuklick, B. (1989). *Paine: Political Writings*. Cambridge, England: Cambridge University Press. p. xix.

[42] Smith, G. H. (2014, April 25). Thomas Paine Versus Edmund Burke, Part 1. Retrieved from https://www.libertarianism.org/columns/thomas-paine-versus-edmund-burke-part-1

that is increase of taxes." The French Revolution became Paine's top priority.[43]

Paine was in favor of the French Revolution. He wrote *The Rights of Man* in two parts. Part one was published on March 13, 1791, and part two was published on February 17, 1792.[44] The book sold an immense number of copies and it might have been the best-selling book ever printed, other than the Bible.[45]

Paine wrote *The Rights of Man* in plain language, with courage and conviction, after becoming infuriated by political theorist and author Edmund Burke. Burke had written a pamphlet, *Reflections on the Revolution in France*, savagely criticizing the French Revolution as a revolt against the monarchy, the elite, and the Established Church.[46]

In *The Rights of Man*, Paine responded:

> The fraud, hypocrisy, and imposition of governments, are now beginning to be too well understood to promise them any long career. The farce of monarchy and aristocracy, in all countries, is following that of chivalry, and Mr. Burke is dressing for the funeral.[47]

The English government countered by putting an order out for Paine's arrest and indicted him for treason. But Paine could not be captured since he was headed to France, having been appointed to a seat in the National Convention. He was tried in absentia and found guilty of seditious libel. *The Rights of Man* was ordered permanently suppressed.[48]

---

[43] Thomas Paine - New World Encyclopedia. (n.d.). Retrieved from http://www.newworldencyclopedia.org/entry/Thomas_Paine

[44] Foner, Thomas Paine.

[45] Smith, G. H. Thomas Paine Versus Edmund Burke, Part 1.

[46] Burke, E. (1897) *Reflections on The Revolution in France*. London: George Bell and Sons. Retrieved from https://archive.org/details/in.ernet.dli.2015.45683/page/n1

[47] Paine, T. (2009). *The Thomas Paine Collection*. New York, Classic Books America. p. 260.

[48] Foner, Thomas Paine.

Why did France need a revolution? The country was run by King Louis XVI, his wife Marie Antoinette, the nobles, and the clergy (also known as the Ancien Régime). French royalty claimed to have a divine right to rule. They lived a luxurious lifestyle and did not pay taxes. People were suffering and starving from food shortages, and France's economy was in collapse.

King Louis XVI was dethroned in 1792 and a republic was declared in France. Louis XVI was tried for treason and sentenced to be executed by guillotine.[49]

Thomas Paine spoke against the execution of Louis, even though the convention had already voted. Paine was filled with true love and compassion: he wanted to destroy the monarchy, not the monarch. He voted for the abolition of tyranny, and against the death of the king.

After Paine spoke out, he was imprisoned.

Believing his life was coming to an end, Paine knew he didn't have a second to waste, so he began writing his thoughts on "organized religion" to share them with the world. He wrote the first part of *The Age of Reason*.[50]

Then he gave the manuscript to his friend Joel Barlow.

Six hours later, Paine was arrested and taken to the Luxembourg prison. Joel Barlow published the first part of *The Age of Reason* in 1794, for a mere three pence, to keep editions widely circulated.[51]

Paine continued to write the second part of *The Age of Reason* while he was in prison.[52]

---

[49] Ten Minute History - The French Revolution and Napoleon (Short Documentary). (2016, September 12). Retrieved from https://youtu.be/NeVJDd1XhIk?t=230

[50] Ingersoll, R. G. *The Complete Works of Robert Ingersoll*, vol. XI, p 331.

[51] Davidson, E. H., & Scheick, W. J. *Paine, Scripture, and Authority: The Age of Reason as Religious and Political Idea*. Lehigh University Press. p.105–106.

[52] Ingersoll, R.G. *The Complete Works of Robert Ingersoll*, vol. XI, p 331.

Paine's detainment in France caused turmoil in America, and future President James Monroe, had to utilize most of his political connections to get Paine released. Paine was set free in November 1794, after ten months and nine days of imprisonment.[53]

The second part of *The Age of Reason* was published in October 1795. Part one and part two were sold together by Francis Place and bookseller Thomas Williams. In 1796, *The Age of Reason* sold 2,000 copies. Williams then produced another copy that he intended on selling for one shilling, but his momentum was broken as The British Government, because the British government feared that *The Age of Reason* would create widespread freethinkers and revolutionary ideas. Williams was indicted, *The Age of Reason* was suppressed, and the British Government began to confiscate copies.[54]

Paine wrote part three of *The Age of Reason,* entitled: *Examination of the Prophecies.* The book compared the Old Testament prophecies and the happening of Jesus Christ in the New Testament. The book was ready for publication in 1802, but Thomas Jefferson discouraged Paine from publishing it because Jefferson feared that it would create a negative response from the public. The book was published five years later, in 1807, entitled: *An Examination of the Passages in the New Testament, quoted from the Old and Called Prophecies Concerning Jesus Christ.*[55]

Paine explains his beliefs about organized religion in the first part of *The Age of Reason*:

> I do not believe in the creed professed by the Jewish church, by the Roman church, by the Greek church, by the Turkish church, by the Protestant church, nor by any church that I know of. My own mind is my own church. All national

---

[53] Editors, H. (2018, December 13). An American hero is arrested in France. Retrieved from https://www.history.com/this-day-in-history/an-american-hero-is-arrested-in-france

[54] Davidson, E. H., & Scheick, W. J. *Paine, Scripture, and Authority.* p. 106.

[55] Davidson, E. H., & Scheick, W. J. *Paine, Scripture, and Authority.* p. 103.

institutions of churches, whether Jewish, Christian, or Turkish, appear to me no other than human inventions, set up to terrify and enslave mankind, and monopolize power and profit.[56]

Paine goes on to talk about the importance of examining the Bible and all forms of organized religion with the utmost strictness as it is supposed to be the Word of God:

> When a book, as is the case with the Old and New Testament, is ushered into the world under the title of being the *Word of God*, it ought to be examined with the utmost strictness, in order to know if it has a well-founded claim to that title or not, and whether we are or are not imposed upon: for no poison is so dangerous as that which poisons the physic, so no falsehood is so fatal as that which is made an article of faith.[57]

When I read Paine's words, they spoke to me clearly, truthfully, and compassionately.

Paine's writings influenced many people to think for themselves rather than dwell in fear and being spoon-fed superstition.

One-person Paine influenced was Robert Ingersoll.

---

[56] Paine, T. (1945) *The Age of Reason*. London: Watts & Co. p. 2.

[57] Paine, T. (1945) *The Age of Reason*. p. 220–221.

ROBERT INGERSOLL

Every mind should be true to itself—should think, investigate and conclude for itself.

—Robert Ingersoll [58]

Robert G. Ingersoll was an American lawyer, Civil War veteran, and political leader. Using his writings and eloquent speeches, Ingersoll relentlessly advocated for justice, liberty, and free thought. He spoke on women's rights, race relations, birth control, capital punishment, and the role of religion in modern state with its authority and control over people's minds.

Ingersoll became known as "The Great Agnostic" for his outspoken criticism of organized religion.

Robert Ingersoll was raised as a devout Christian. His father, John Ingersoll, was a Congregationalist minister. Robert Ingersoll began to question the Bible after his father was charged with prevarication for having liberal views opposed to those of other members of his church.

John Ingersoll's ministerial career was shut down by a church trial that occurred while he was pastor of the Congregational Church at Madison, Ohio, when young Robert was nine years old. The committee that heard the trial decided that, even though John Ingersoll had done "nothing inconsistent with his Christian character," he was "inconsistent with his ministerial character," and forbade him to

---

[58] Ingersoll, R. G. *The Complete Works of Robert G. Ingersoll*, vol. 1, p. 179.

preach in the future.[59]

This made Robert Ingersoll question Christianity in all forms. It inspired him to relentlessly study and write his opinions on the Christian doctrine. He spoke out against the Bible's irrational thought, superstition, and opposition to women's rights, and the fear it puts into people's minds and hearts.[60]

In Ingersoll's writings I found an electrifying confirmation of my doubts about the Bible:

> It declared that all other religions were false and infamous…. Thought was its enemy, obedience was its friend. Investigation was fraught with danger; therefore investigation was suppressed.[61]

> In short, Christianity has always opposed every forward movement of the human race. Across the highway of progress, it has always been building breastworks of Bibles, tracts, commentaries, prayer-books, creeds, dogmas and platforms, and at every advance the Christians have gathered together behind these heaps of rubbish and shot the poisoned arrows of malice at the soldiers of freedom.[62]

> Superstition, the mother of those hideous twins, Fear and Faith, from her throne of skulls, still rules the world, and will until the mind of woman ceases to be the property of priests. When women reason, and babes sit in the lap of philosophy, the victory of reason over the shadowy host of darkness will be complete.[63]

---

[59] Wilson. R, R. (March 16, 1890) A Sketch of the Life of America's Most Noted Agnostic Part 1. The Elmira Telegram. Retrieved from http://www.crookedlakereview.com/articles/34_66/41aug1991/41wilson.html

[60] Ingersoll, R. G. *The Works of Robert G. Ingersoll, Complete Contents by Robert Green Ingersoll - Free Ebook*. Retrieved from http://www.gutenberg.org/files/38813/38813-h/38813-h.htm

[61] Ingersoll, R.G. *The Complete Works of Robert G. Ingersoll*, vol. 1, p. 193.

[62] *The Complete Works of Robert G. Ingersoll*, vol. 1. pp. 193-194

[63] *The Complete Works of Robert G. Ingersoll*, vol. 1. pp. 195-196.

It unfortunately goes without saying that Ingersoll's books were banned from libraries and his speeches were regularly disrupted. But he had a profound influence on many people during his time prompting them to think rationally and question the Church and its divine power.[64]

Among the people he influenced were the Wright brothers.

---

[64] Ingersoll, R. G., & Page, T. (2005). *What's God Got to Do with It?: Robert G. Ingersoll on Free Thought, Honest Talk, and the Separation of Church and State.* Hanover, NH: Steerforth. p. 4.

THE WRIGHT BROTHERS

Wilbur and Orville Wright were the children of Reverend Milton Wright, a United Brethren Bishop, and his wife, Susan. They had two older brothers, Reuchlin and Lorin, and a younger sister, Katherine. They lived in Kitty Hawk, North Carolina.[65]

The Wright Brothers were very fortunate that their father encouraged his family to read books. One author they were encouraged to read was "The Great Agnostic," Robert Ingersoll. Ingersoll taught them that "Every mind should be true to itself—should, think, investigate and conclude for itself." According to David McCullough's book *The Wright Brothers*, Ingersoll's influence led the brothers to give up regular attendance at church.[66]

The Wright brothers did not wait for the God of the Bible to take them to Heaven. They decided to go there themselves—or at least to get up into the sky. They started working on building a machine that would let humans fly.

Other people in Kitty Hawk did not think that was right. William Tate, the local postmaster, told them so. In McCullough's book, Tate recalls: "We believed in a good God, a bad Devil, and a hot Hell, and more than anything else we believed that same God did not intend man should ever fly."[67]

---

[65] The Wright Family. (n.d.). Retrieved from http://www.wright-brothers.org/Information_Desk/Just_the_Facts/Wright_Family/Wright_Family.htm

[66] McCullough, D., *The Wright Brothers* (New York: Simon & Schuster, 2016), p. 17.

[67] McCullough, D., *The Wright Brothers*. p. 48.

The Wright brothers did not care. They were not going to wait to be angels before they could have wings. They worked relentlessly, six days a week on a small budget to accomplish what the Church deemed to be impossible.

Then on December 17, 1903, the brothers fearlessly achieved their goal with a flight twenty feet above the ground, lasting twelve seconds and covering a distance of 120 feet.[68]

Today we can fly around the world and send people into space. The God of the Bible and His fearful believers would have kept us stuck in the sand. Of course, even conservative Christians take airplanes today, with very few exceptions.

But if the Wright brothers first gave us flight, who gave us light?

Most people will tell you Thomas Edison did. But I learned that we owe the light, warmth, power, and technology in our homes and lives to the freethinking inventor and animal rights activist Nikola Tesla. I also learned that, in a way, I owe my life to him.

---

[68] The Wright Brothers - First Flight, 1903. (n.d.). Retrieved from http://www.eyewitnesstohistory.com/wright.htm

NIKOLA TESLA

I read Marc J. Seifer's great book *Wizard: The Life and Times of Nikola Tesla: Biography of a Genius*. The incredible book took Seifer seventeen years of daily work to complete.[69] I read and listened to the masterpiece several times and learned that Tesla was indefatigable, relentless, and one of the most important people to ever live.

Nikola Tesla was a Serbian-American inventor born at the stroke of midnight between July 9 and 10, 1856, in the village of Smiljan, Croatia.[70]

Tesla invented the alternating current (AC) induction motor. The alternating current induction motor enabled electricity to travel hundreds of miles. Before Tesla's invention, Thomas Edison's direct current was being used. But with direct current, you needed to be within two kilometers of a power station, because electricity loses energy as it travels through the wires. Direct current also carried significantly less power, and it only had the ability to illuminate dwellings.

Tesla also invented the electrical power distribution system, fluorescent and neon light, remote control, robotics, and wireless communication.[71]

---

[69] Phone interview with Marc J. Seifer. January 2019.

[70] Cheney, M. (1981). *Tesla: Man Out of Time*. New York, NY: Touchstone, p. 25.

[71] Seifer, M. J. (1996) *The Life and Times of Nikola Tesla*. New York, NY: Kensington Publishing Corp. p. xi.

My parents met when my dad was attending Humber College and taking a course in radio.

You could say that without Tesla's AC induction motor and wireless communication inventions, I would not have been born.

When I read this, I knew that a God in the sky did not choose for me to be born as my Sunday school teachers had preached. Nikola Tesla did not create me or intend for me to be born, either, but he helped create opportunity that enabled my parents to meet, get married, and conceive my sister and me. Tesla also helped create the warm, comfortable environment I grew up in.

Tesla did not grow up in such an environment.

His father, Milutin Tesla, was a Serbian Orthodox priest. Nikola Tesla said:

> Up to the age of eight years my character was weak and vacillating… I was oppressed by thoughts of pain in life and death and religious fear…I was swayed by superstitious belief and lived in constant dread of the spirit of evil, of ghosts and ogres and other unholy monsters of the dark.[72]

Then Tesla had a life-changing experience. He broke his father's rules and read the book that changed his life forever.

> All at once, there came a tremendous change which altered the course of my whole existence. Of all things, I liked books the best. My father had a large library and whenever I could manage I tried to satisfy my passion for reading. He did not permit it and would fly into a rage when he caught me in the act. He hid the candles when he found that I was reading in secret. He did not want me to spoil my eyes. But I obtained tallow, made the wicking and cast the sticks into tin forms,

---

[72] Tesla, N. (1919, February). My Inventions. *The Electrical Experimenter Science and Invention.* p. 746.

> and every night I would bush the keyhole and the cracks and read, often till dawn, when all others slept and my mother started on her arduous daily task. On one occasion, I came across a novel entitled *Abafi (the Son of Aba)*, a Serbian translation of a well-known Hungarian writer, Josika. This work somehow awakened my dormant powers of will and I began to practice self-control. At first my resolutions faded like snow in April, but in a little while I conquered my weakness and left a pleasure I never knew before—that of doing as I willed.[73]

With that thought Tesla became enlightened and wanted to make the world a better place, unconditionally. He learned to care for all those we share the world with, including non-human animals.

Tesla recommended a plant-based diet.

> It is certainly preferable to raise vegetables, and I think, therefore, that vegetarianism is a commendable departure from the established barbarous habit. That we can subsist on plant food and perform our work even to advantage is not a theory, but a well-demonstrated fact. Many races living almost exclusively on vegetables are of superior physique and strength.…Every effort should be made to stop the wanton and cruel slaughter of animals, which must be destructive to our morals. To free ourselves from animal instincts and appetites, which keep us down, we should begin at the very root from which we spring: we should effect a radical reform in the character of the food.[74]

Tesla knew it was wrong to participate in torturing and killing animals.

---

[73] Tesla, N. (1919, February). My Inventions. *The Electrical Experimenter Science and Invention*. p. 746.

[74] Tesla, N., *The Problem of Increasing Human Energy with Special References to the Harnessing of the Sun's Energy*, retrieved from https://archive.org/details/TeslaProblemEnergy/page/n9

Tesla's words had a lasting impact on me. I began to uncover the savage truth about the animal agriculture industry, and it influenced me to go vegan and become a human and animal rights activist. I remember Tesla's great words at slaughterhouses, marches, posting on the internet about animal exploitation, and any other form of activism that I do: "Every effort should be made to stop the wanton and cruel slaughter of animals which must be destructive to our morals."[75]

I realized Tesla was one of the greatest people to ever live and I knew he must have been following someone great.

I discovered Tesla was a follower of Swami Vivekananda. He met Vivekananda at his lectures in the 1890s and learned concepts that helped him to describe the physics of the universe and the creation of matter.[76]

---

[75] Tesla, N., *The Problem of Increasing Human Energy with Special References to the Harnessing of the Sun's Energy*.

[76] Press, S., & Frank, S. J, T. (Writers), & Miracle, J. (Director). (1998, December 11). Lost lightning the missing secrets of Nikola Tesla. [Television series episode]. R. Uth (Producer), *Phenomenon: The Lost Archives*. Retrieved from https://youtu.be/Kh7y4SZhRKk?t=2375

SWAMI VIVEKANANDA

Swami Vivekananda was a Hindu monk and philosopher who lived during the nineteenth century. He was one of the most famous and influential spiritual leaders of the philosophies of Vedanta and Yoga. He was an amazing person who founded the Ramakrishna Mission in 1897, which became the largest charity in India.[77]

Vivekananda gave a speech in Chicago on September 20, 1893, at the Parliament of the World's Religions. When I read it, the memories of the horrific poverty and orphan children that I had seen in the Philippines came back to me.

It spoke directly to me.

> You Christians, who are so fond of sending out missionaries to save the soul of the heathen—why do you not try to save their bodies from starvation? In India, during the terrible famines, thousands died from hunger, yet you Christians did nothing. You erect churches all through India, but the crying evil in the East is not religion—they have religion enough—but it is bread that the suffering millions of burning India cry out for with parched throats. They ask us for bread, but we give them stones. It is an insult to a starving people to offer them religion; it is an insult to a starving man to teach him metaphysics. In India a priest that preached for money would lose caste and be spat upon by the people. I came here to

---

[77] RKMSVH | History. (n.d.). Retrieved from http://www.vivekanandahome.org/cms_pages.php?page_id=21

seek aid for my impoverished people, and I fully realised how difficult it was to get help for heathens from Christians in a Christian land.[78]

I connected the dots when I read Vivekananda's speech.

Christianity, I concluded, as an institution, cares only for itself and its own perpetuation.

The church Our Lady of the Atonement Cathedral in Baguio, as well as many others in Metro Manila, were examples of Christians building prestigious churches while poverty-stricken individuals suffered around them.

Vivekananda's truth gave me momentum. It led me at last to Bertrand Russell, who, famously, was not a Christian.

---

[78] Vivekananda. S. The Complete Works of Swami Vivekananda/Volume 1/Addresses at The Parliament of Religions/Religion not the Crying need of India - Wikisource, the free online library. (n.d.). Retrieved from
https://en.wikisource.org/wiki/The_Complete_Works_of_Swami_Vivekananda/Volume_1/Addresses_at_The_Parliament_of_Religions/Religion_not_the_Crying_need_of_India

BERTRAND RUSSELL

Bertrand Russell was a British philosopher, mathematician, writer, and political activist. He was awarded the Nobel Prize in Literature in 1950.[79]

In 1927, Russell gave a lecture, "Why I Am Not a Christian." [80] The lecture was later published as a pamphlet and has been republished in English and translation.

When I listened to it, I understood why the Sunday school teachers taught me to live in fear, why the Bible was based on fear, why the townsfolk of Toulouse acted with such fear and hatred, and why so many people who had done great things had broken away from the Church to do them:

> Religion is based, I think, primarily and mainly upon fear. It is partly the terror of the unknown…Fear is the basis of the whole thing. Fear of the mysterious, fear of defeat, fear of death. Fear is the parent of cruelty, and therefore it is no wonder cruelty and religion have gone hand-in-hand. It is because fear is at the basis of those two things.[81]

After listening to Russell, I remembered what my Sunday school

---

[79] The Nobel prize in literature 1950. (n.d.). Retrieved from https://www.nobelprize.org/prizes/literature/1950/summary

[80] Why I Am Not a Christian by Bertrand Russell. Retrieved from https://youtu.be/0F6J8o7AAe8?t=2142

[81] Russell, B. (1957). *Why I Am Not a Christian: And Other Essays on Religion and Related Subjects*. New York, NY: Simon & Schuster. p. 22.

teacher had said: that you had to believe in Jesus or else you go to a place of darkness, fire, and lava. I remembered how the townspeople of Kitty Hawk believed that the Wright brothers should not invade the realm of their "ally in the sky."

Has religion put fear into your mind?

Christians, of course, will not agree that their religion is based on fear. They will tell you it is based on love and compassion. If I point to Voltaire, Paine, Ingersoll, Vivekananda, and Russell, they will point to Mother Teresa.

Is Mother Teresa the answer to my concerns? Does she refute all that I have learned about the Church, about Christianity, about religion?

I knew I had to find out.

I was shocked by what I discovered.

MOTHER TERESA

Mother Teresa was born Agnes Gonxha Bojaxhiu in Skopje (now the capital of Macedonia), Ottoman Empire. Her parents, Nikola and Dranafile Bojaxhiu, were devout Catholics.

Her father passed away when she was about eight years old. Her father's death had a major impact on their family, both emotionally and financially. Agnes's religious beliefs strengthened in the Jesuit parish of the Sacred Heart, where she was very involved. At age eighteen she moved to Ireland and joined the Institute of the Blessed Virgin Mary, known as the Sisters of Loreto. She received the name Sister Mary Teresa after St. Thérèse of Lisieux.

In December 1928, Sister Teresa left Ireland; she arrived in Calcutta (now called Kolkata) on January 6, 1929 and taught at a school for girls. On May 24, 1937, Sister Teresa made her Final Profession of Vows, becoming, as she said, the "spouse of Jesus" for "all eternity." From that moment on she was known as Mother Teresa.

Mother Teresa experienced the "call within a call." She was going from Calcutta to the Himalayan foothills for a retreat when she claimed Christ spoke to her and explained that she must abandon teaching. Christ then told her to go to Calcutta to serve the poorest, most disadvantaged, and sickest people in the slums of Calcutta.[82]

---

[82] Mother Teresa of Calcutta (1910-1997), biography. (n.d.). Retrieved from http://www.vatican.va/news_services/liturgy/saints/ns_lit_doc_20031019_madre-teresa_en.html

When I read this, I was skeptical of her being chosen among billions of people on the planet. But however she got there, she was helping poor people.

Wasn't she?

"Please tell Jesus to stop kissing me."

In 2008, Hemley Gonzalez, a migrant from Cuban living in Miami, running a real estate business became inspired after reading a biography of Mother Teresa. He went to Kolkata to serve at Nirmal Hriday, a home for the dying run by the Mother Teresa's Missionaries of Charity. He stayed for two months.

"It was a scene out of a World War II concentration camp," Gonzalez recalls.

"I was shocked to see the negligence. Needles were washed in cold water and reused and expired medicines were given to the inmates. There were people who had a chance to live if given proper care."[83]

When Gonzalez tried to suggest improvements, such as a water heater, he was denied.

"We don't do that here. This is the way Jesus wants it," he was told.[84]

Why would this world-famous charity mission, dedicated to caring for the poor, keep people in these conditions?

I had to know.

I watched a video by Penn Jillette and Teller featuring Dr. Aroup

---

[83] Thomas, P. M. (2013, June 19). Pointing Fingers At Mother Teresa's Heirs. Retrieved from https://www.forbes.com/2010/08/10/forbes-india-mother-teresa-charity-critical-public-review.html#4bcfe78c108e

[84] Burke, D. Mother Teresa's supporters defend her legacy ahead of sainthood. (2016, September 1). Retrieved from https://www.dailymail.co.uk/news/article-3768844/We-don-t-prove-saints-perfect-Mother-Teresa-s-supporters-defend-legacy-just-days-Pope-makes-saint-amid-accusations-revelled-misery-poor.html

Chatterjee, a British Indian author born in Kolkata.[85] He has done research on Mother Teresa for more than twenty-five years and is the author of the book *Mother Teresa: The Untold Story*.[86]

Penn and Teller showed footage from Mother Teresa's home for the dying in Kolkata. People were living in small hammocks, suffering in horrific conditions. Dr. Chatterjee described it: "There is a communal toilet that people have to defecate in the presence of each other. They are not allowed visits from their friends or relatives. Very strange. They have to lie in the bed or sit in the bed consistently."[87]

I had thought that Mother Teresa was there to help relieve poverty and suffering. Instead, I was appalled to learn that she praised poverty and believed that suffering was a way to get closer to Jesus.

This woman, who has been called a "living saint," once told a woman suffering from terrible pain and dying from cancer, "This terrible pain is but the kiss of Jesus—a sign that you have come so close to Jesus on the cross that he can kiss you."

The woman joined her hands together and said, "Mother Teresa, please tell Jesus to stop kissing me."[88]

I had always thought that Mother Teresa was there to comfort the poor. But it seemed that pain was all she had to offer. I kept seeking to learn more.

In the early hours of December 3, 1984, poisonous gas leaked and oozed from a pesticide plant owned by the chemical company Union

---

[85] Jillette, P., & Teller (Writers), & Price, S. (Director). (2005, May 23). [Television series episode]. In E. Nicholas (Producer), *Penn & Teller: Bullshit!. Holier Than Thou.* (TV Episode 2005). (2005, May 23). Retrieved from https://youtu.be/V4nCaxHN-cY

[86] Chatterjee, A. (2016). *Mother Teresa: The Untold Story*. New Delhi: Prakash Book Depot.

[87] *Penn & Teller: Bullshit! Holier Than Thou.* Retrieved from https://youtu.be/V4nCaxHN-cY?t=343

[88] Blessed Mother Teresa of Calcutta tell Jesus stop kissing. (2008, February 9). Retrieved from https://youtu.be/IkIyQyrfQS4?t=41

Carbide in the Indian city of Bhopal. The toxic gas stayed low to the ground, seeping into the eyes of victims, burning their throats, killing thousands, and leaving more than half a million people with serious, long-term, health problems. After this horrific tragedy occurred, Mother Teresa went to Bhopal.[89]

Mother Teresa arrived at the scene and announced "Forgive, forgive" to the suffering victims. She repeated herself, then vanished from the scene of the worst industrial disaster in history.

If Mother Teresa were a saint, she would have been doing everything she could to help. She could have provided, food, water, and shelter for the victims. The Missionaries of Charity had a small home in Bhopal that could have helped.

Be that as it may, they did practically nothing. Mother Teresa did visit patients in clinics, and she offered her prayers and blossoms while posturing for the global media.[90]

Mother Teresa once said that when she was in trouble, she would "cling to Christ, because he is the only answer."[91] Thousands of people perished, and hundreds of thousands continue to have serious long-term health problems from the gas explosion in Bhopal. The water is still contaminated in Bhopal and people continue to have sick and deformed children.[92]

Her "clinging to Christ" has not changed that. Could it be that this famous charity simply did not have the means to help? That Teresa's vows of poverty meant that her charity did not have money?

---

[89] Storm, C. (2014, December 5). Protests Rage in India On The Anniversary Of The Bhopal Disaster. Retrieved from https://www.businessinsider.in/Protests-Rage-In-India-On-The-Anniversary-Of-The-Bhopal-Disaster/articleshow/45379420.cms

[90] Chatterjee, *Mother Teresa The Untold Story*, p. 19.

[91] Mother Teresa of Calcutta on Irish Television, (1974, September 15,) Retrieved from https://www.youtube.com/watch?v=Th2QzJwy8tI&feature=youtu.be&t=1445

[92] Storm, C. Business Insider, *Protests Rage in India on the Anniversary of the Bhopal Disaster.*

I soon learned that it had more than enough.

"Mother was very concerned that we preserve our spirit of poverty."

Gianluigi Nuzzi, Italian television host, journalist, and best-selling author,[93] had access to documents revealing Mother Teresa's secret account at the IOR (short for Istituto per le Opere di Religione, Institute for the Works of Religion, commonly known as the Vatican Bank).

In Nuzzi's book, *The Original Sin*, he confirms that Mother Teresa was believed to have "by far the most cashed-up account" at the Vatican Bank.[94]

Nuzzi writes, "The balance remains one of the best kept secrets at IOR." He adds, "If only Mother Teresa had closed the accounts or transferred them, the institution would have risked default."[95]

How could this be? An article by Susan Shields gave me more answers.

Susan Shields served as a Missionaries of Charity sister for almost ten years as Sister Virgin at the houses in San Francisco, Rome, and New York. Her job was to record donations to the Missionaries of Charity and write the thank-you letters. She recalls how it was:

> The money arrived at a frantic rate. The mail carrier often delivered the letters in sacks. We wrote receipts for checks of $50,000 and more on a regular basis. Sometimes a donor would call up and ask if we had received his check, expecting us to remember it readily because it was so large. How could

---

[93] About me - Gianluigi Nuzzi Blog. (n.d.). Retrieved from http://www.gianluiginuzzi.com/mi-presento/?lang=en

[94] 'Cashed-up' Mother Teresa kept Vatican Bank afloat — journalist. (n.d.). Retrieved from https://www.rt.com/news/409393-mother-teresa-bank-account

[95] Vaticano, nuovo libro di Nuzzi: dagli abusi al super conto Ior di Madre Teresa. (n.d.). Retrieved from https://www.lapresse.it/cronaca/vaticano_nuovo_libro_di_nuzzi_dagli_abusi_al_super_conto_ior_di_madre_teresa-132632/news/2017-11-09

we say that we could not recall it because we had received so many that were even larger?

When Mother spoke publicly, she never asked for money, but she did encourage people to make sacrifices for the poor, to "give until it hurts." Many people did—and they gave it to her. We received touching letters from people, sometimes apparently poor themselves, who were making sacrifices to send us a little money for the starving people in Africa, the flood victims in Bangladesh, or the poor children in India. Most of the money sat in our bank accounts... Our bank account was already the size of a great fortune and increased with every postal service delivery. Around $50 million had collected in one checking account in the Bronx

... For years I had to write thousands of letters to donors, telling them that their entire gift would be used to bring God's loving compassion to the poorest of the poor. I was able to keep my complaining conscience in check because we had been taught that the Holy Spirit was guiding Mother.

But how was it guiding her? What did Mother Teresa believe the Holy Spirit was telling her to do? Just as she believed that suffering was the kiss of Jesus, she believed that God wanted her, her missionaries, and all the people she served to be poor. Even if they had uncountable millions, they were still to have a "spirit of poverty."

The donations rolled in and were deposited in the bank, but they had no effect on our ascetic lives and very little effect on the lives of the poor we were trying to help... Mother was very concerned that we preserve our spirit of poverty. Spending money would destroy that poverty.[96]

---

[96] © 1997 The Council for Secular Humanism. This article originally appeared in *Free Inquiry* magazine, volume 18, number 1 (Winter 1997/1998).

It was not that she didn't want to receive money. Mother Teresa believed and told people the Lord was sending money to her. "Money…I never think of it. It always comes. The Lord sends it. We do His work; He provides the means. If He does not give us the means, that shows He does not want the work."[97]

She wanted the money as a sign from God. She wanted people to give. But she didn't want to spend the money. She didn't want to give it to others. She wanted everyone to be in poverty.

I remembered the children starving outside of Catholic churches in the Philippines and I realized that this is what the Catholic Church wanted.

But when this woman who told her followers that suffering is the kiss of Jesus became ill herself, she received first-class medical treatment. In 1991, Mother Teresa went to Scripps Hospital in San Diego where Dr. Paul Tierstein, recognized worldwide as a leader in interventional cardiology, performed a life-saving operation.[98]

Why did Mother Teresa not want to come closer to Jesus through suffering?

"Ask yourself what Jesus would do?"

I wondered where Mother Teresa's true definition of the Lord's money was truthfully coming from. On further research, I learned she was accepting money from criminals.

Mother Teresa accepted at least $1.25 million from Charles Keating, a corrupt American banker who stole at least $253 million. Over 21,000 elderly people lost their entire life savings when his financial empire

---

[97] Kaufman, M. T. (1979, December 9). THE WORLD OF MOTHER TERESA; MOTHER TERESA. Retrieved from https://www.nytimes.com/1979/12/09/archives/the-world-of-mother-teresa-mother-teresa.html

[98] San Diego doctor saved Mother Teresa's life. (2016, September 2). Retrieved from https://www.youtube.com/watch?v=QIsNOkL3Mow

went bankrupt.[99]

Bill Donahue, the president of the Catholic League for Religious and Civil Rights, knew that Teresa accepted money from Charles Keating, and his response was, "When she got the money from Charles Keating, he hadn't been indicted about anything. He hadn't even been accused of anything, so what was she supposed to do? The money was already spent by the time that they found out that this guy was a crook."[100]

It would be one thing if she accepted money and never knew that it was stolen. But Mother Teresa knew Keating was a fraud and refused to return the stolen funds to the rightful owners. What's more, we now know that she had far more than that much just sitting in her bank accounts.

After Keating was convicted and sentenced to prison, Paul W. Turley, the co-prosecutor, wrote the following letter to Mother Teresa asking her to return the stolen money she had unjustly received:

> Dear Mother Teresa:
>
> ...Mr. Keating was convicted of defrauding 17 individuals of more than $900,000. These 17 persons were representative of 17,000 individuals from whom Mr. Keating stole $252,000,000.
>
> ....One was, indeed a poor carpenter who did not speak English and had his life savings stolen by Mr Keating's fraud...Ask yourself what Jesus would do if given the fruits of a crime; what Jesus would do if he were in possession of money that had been stolen...I submit that Jesus would

---

[99] Nickolas, M. (2017, December 6). 20 Years Later: Another McCain At Center of a Bank Collapse and Government Take-Over? Retrieved from https://www.huffingtonpost.com/mark-nickolas/20-years-later-another-mc_b_115380.html

[100] *Penn & Teller: Bullshit! Holier Than Thou*. Retrieved from https://youtu.be/V4nCaxHN-cY?t=205.

promptly and unhesitatingly return the stolen property to its rightful owners. You should do the same. You have been given money by Mr Keating that he has been convicted of stealing by fraud... Do not keep the money. Return it to those who worked for it and earned it!

If you contact me, I will put you in direct contact with the rightful owners of the property now in your possession.

Sincerely

Paul W. Turley

Three years later, Mr. Turley has received no reply to his letter. Nor can anybody account for the missing money: saints, it seems, are immune to audit. [101]

Did Mother Teresa even care about the moral character of her supporters?

In 1981, Mother Teresa traveled to Haiti to accept the Légion d'Honneur award from the Duvalier family. The Duvaliers ran Haiti as a dictatorship. People in Haiti lived in terror and poverty, as the Duvaliers and their followers controlled all of Haiti's wealth. Anyone caught disobeying or questioning the Duvalier regime was bullied, kidnapped, tortured, or murdered. [102]

The Duvaliers were responsible for the deaths of over 30,000 of their own people between 1957 and 1986. [103]

---

[101] Hitchens, C. (1995). *The Missionary Position: Mother Teresa in Theory and Practice*. Brooklyn, NY: Verso. p. 70-71.

[102] Jean-Bertrand Aristide Biography - life, family, children, parents, history, school, young, son, old, information, born. (n.d.). Retrieved from https://www.notablebiographies.com/news/A-Ca/Aristide-Jean-Bertrand.html#ixzz5VRzbo2vl

[103] Second Thought. (2016, October 14). *The Unfortunate Truth About Mother Teresa* [Video file]. Retrieved from https://www.youtube.com/watch?v=2uxtcy4FpN8&feature=youtu.be&t=278https://www.youtube.com/watch?v=2uxtcy4FpN8&feature=youtu.be&t=278

I was learning a very ugly lesson about Mother Teresa, her charity, and the Catholic Church.

What do you think about Mother Teresa accepting money from and being acquainted with criminals and dictators?

"I'm not a social worker. I do it for the church."

At last I found the work of Christopher Hitchens. Hitchens was a world-renowned author. He wrote a book, *The Missionary Position*, critiquing and challenging Mother Teresa's work, and he co-wrote and starred in the documentary *Hell's Angel* about Mother Teresa's deceitful life.[104]

In *Hell's Angel*, Mary London, a former volunteer at the Missionaries of Charity House, describes a boy being denied a hospital visit when he was sick and dying:

> First day I was there when I'd finished working in the women's ward, I went and waited on the edge of the men's ward for my boyfriend, who was looking after a boy, fifteen, who was dying, and an American doctor told me that she had been trying to treat this boy. And that he had a really a relatively simple kidney complaint that had simply got worse and worse and worse because he hadn't had antibiotics, and he actually needed an operation. I don't recall what the problem was, she did tell me. And she was so angry, but also very resigned, which so many people become in that situation. She said, "Well, they won't take him to hospital." And I said "Why? All you have to do is get a cab, take him to the nearest hospital, demand that he has treatment, get him an operation." She said, "They don't do it, they won't do it. If

---

[104] Hitchens, C. (Writer), & Morgan, J. (Director). (1994, November 8). Hell's Angel [Television broadcast]. A. Tariq (Producer), UK: Channel 4.

they do it for one they do it for everybody." And I thought, but this kid's fifteen.[105]

Missionaries of Charity had millions of dollars. There was no reason to deny anyone a hospital visit. At least there was no good, compassionate reason.

Christopher Hitchens had the opportunity to meet and speak with Mother Teresa:

> She lied to donors about how their contributions were used. "It was by talking to her that I discovered, and she assured me, that she wasn't working to alleviate poverty," he said. "She was working to expand the number of Catholics. She said, 'I'm not a social worker. I don't do it for this reason. I do it for Christ. I do it for the church.'"[106]

When Mother Teresa was given the Nobel Prize, she said in her acceptance speech,

> Let us here make a strong resolution, we are going to save every little child, every unborn child, give them a chance to be born. And what we are doing, we are fighting abortion by adoption, and the good God has blessed the work so beautifully that we have saved thousands of children, and thousands of children have found a home where they are loved, they are wanted, they are cared.[107]

The Missionaries of Charity sold children.

---

[105] Hell's Angel. Retrieved from https://youtu.be/NJG-lgmPvYA

[106] Leung, R. (2003, October 19). The Debate Over Sainthood. Retrieved from https://www.cbsnews.com/news/the-debate-over-sainthood

[107] The Nobel Peace Prize 1979. (n.d.). Retrieved from https://www.nobelprize.org/prizes/peace/1979/teresa/26200-mother-teresa-acceptance-speech-1979

"They are not true. They're all lies."

One year after Mother Teresa won her Nobel Prize, in 1980, the Missionaries of Charity sold a young boy named Sonaton Dhar to a Belgian Catholic couple for 125,000 rupees after falsifying his documents.

He and his sisters came from an impoverished family. His father sold ice cream and would sometimes be gone for a week at a time. His mother was often sick at the hospital, leaving Sonaton and his two sisters alone for days without food. He had to look after himself and his sisters when he was only six or seven years old.

Sonaton's mother was admitted to the Mother Teresa Hospice in Prem Dan due to her failing health, and Sonaton and his sisters Shanto and Shontoshi stayed there with her. One month later, his mother passed away. Sonaton and his sisters were listed as "orphans" and sold to Belgian Catholics by the nuns at the hospice while their father, grandmother, and eldest sister, Marani were all still alive.[108]

Do you think that it is right to sell children?

Sonatons name has since changed to Sonaton Pauwels. He is an aeronautical engineer at an Airport in Belgium. He was given a lot, but he is upset about being illegally put up for adoption:

Since 1993, Sonaton Pauwels has been searching for his family, asking the Missionaries of Charity for their help. Sonaton claims he has tried ten to twenty times and some sisters tried to help but he believes they are withholding information about the whereabouts of his family.[109]

Sonaton went to the Missionaries of Charity orphanage in 2002 and found his papers with his photo, but his data was falsified. He

---

[108] Chatterjee, *Mother Teresa: The Untold Story.* p. 211.

[109] *The Truth about Mother Teresa –. The YouTube video has a mistake in its title, His correct name Sonaton Pauwels.* Retrieved from https://youtu.be/pJ1AZSIcswc?t=785

discovered that he was listed as an "orphan" with a statement revealing that his grandmother gave him up for adoption, which is illegal in India. Not only that: neither Sonatons father nor his grandmother wanted him to be adopted.[110]

Sonaton was often visited by his grandmother while staying at the Mother Teresa home, but she was never allowed to enter because, according to Sonaton, the Mother Teresa home did not permit it.[111]

Sonaton has held reunions in Belgium with children who have been illegally adopted. They speak about the problems of adoption and the Mother Teresa Homes without their adopted parents present.[112] Sonaton says once seventy people came to his reunion and most of them miss their families in India.[113] They want to find their birth families because they have problems with their adopted parents in Belgium.

They go to the Mother Teresa House trying to find their biological parents and most times they receive negative news, according to Sonaton. The Mother Teresa Homes tell them their father and mother is dead. "They are not true," Sonaton says. "They're all lies."[114]

The Missionaries of Charity was selling children.

It still is.

In early July 2018, Head nun Sister Concilia, and charity worker Anima Indwar were arrested for selling a child at the Nirmal Hriday,

---

[110] Chatterjee, *Mother Teresa: The Untold Story*. pp. 211–212.

[111] *The Truth about Mother Teresa- Sanatan Powell's Narrative* [Video file]. (2014, February 16). Retrieved from https://youtu.be/pJ1AZSIcswc?t=785

[112] *The Truth about Mother Teresa* [Video file]. (2014, February 16). Retrieved from https://youtu.be/pJ1AZSIcswc?t=1244

[113] *The Truth about Mother Teresa* [Video file]. (2014, February 16). Retrieved from https://youtu.be/pJ1AZSIcswc?t=1266

[114] *The Truth about Mother Teresa* [Video file]. (2014, February 16). Retrieved from https://youtu.be/pJ1AZSIcswc?t=1270

Missionaries of Charity home. The Missionaries of Charity home provides shelter to rescued and pregnant, unmarried woman. The home is in Jharkhand, in northeast India. [115]

In early July 2018, the Bishop of the Archdiocese of Ranchi, Theodore Mascarenhas, was interviewed by Indrajit Kundu from India Today. The interview occurred after Sister Concilia and Anima Indwar had been arrested. During the interview, Bishop Theodore Mascarenhas said that the Missionaries of Charity sisters are "simple holy women trying to do compassion", [116] and he condemned Anima Indwar, pinning all the blame on her:

> Every organization is human, okay. In a human organization, there'll always be one person who can let you down. And Anima Indwar, I think, has let the Missionaries of Charity down. [117]

Bishop Theodore Mascarenhas also stated that the Missionaries of Charity Sisters had nothing to do with the act of selling babies illegally.

> First and foremost, let's make one thing clear. The Missionaries of Charity, Mother Teresa's sisters as we fondly call them, are not at all involved, in this what happened, as an organization, as a congregation. Let me make that very, very clear. There is some vested interest who want to destroy their credibility, and I think that is very unfair to them. [118]

Sunita Kumar, a spokesperson for the Missionaries of Charity came on

---

[115] Kumar, H. (2018, July 6). *Baby Was Sold at Indian Shelter Tied to Mother Teresa, Police Say* - The New York Times. Retrieved from https://www.nytimes.com/2018/07/06/world/asia/india-baby-mother-teresa.html

[116] India Today, *Ranchi Bishop Exclusive on Child Trafficking Charges Against Missionaries of Charity* [Video file]. (2018, July 11). Retrieved from https://youtu.be/pqbhgdlCJ-c?t=423

[117] India Today, *Ranchi Bishop Exclusive on Child Trafficking Charges Against Missionaries of Charity* [Video file]. (2018, July 11). Retrieved from https://youtu.be/pqbhgdlCJ-c?t=157

[118] India Today, *Ranchi Bishop Exclusive on Child Trafficking Charges Against Missionaries of Charity* [Video file]. (2018, July 11). Retrieved from https://youtu.be/pqbhgdlCJ-c?t=70

television in early July 2018, carrying a piece of paper that she said was given to her by Bishop Theodore Mescarenhas. Kumar then read the paper aloud.

> I'm just going to read out a message... I've been told to do this. Bishop Theodore Mascarenhas, who's from Delhi and secretary CBCI, has made a statement... This is a deliberate attempt to malign one of the world's, and India's most loved institutions. Mother Teresa's Missionaries of Charity. The truth will come out.

Kumar then repeats herself by saying, "I've been told to just do this." She then says, "I'm not allowed to say another word".[119] The fact that Sunita Kumar, the spokesperson for the Missionaries of Charity, was not permitted to speak on NDTV is very strange.

Why do you think Bishop Theodore Mascarenhas gave Sunita Kumar a piece of paper with instructions telling her what to say? Why do you think Sunita Kumar was not given permission to speak for herself on television?

The truth did come out.

The Jharkhand Police released a video of Sister Concilia confessing that she sold multiple children, and she also confessed to giving another baby away for free.[120] The video was recorded in Hindi and was translated to English.

Sister Concilia: "Only me, Karishma, and Anima knew about this."

Police officer: "So you three people were involved in this sale? ... Say something!"

Police officer: "How many more kids have you sold?"

---

[119] NDTV. *Crackdown On 'Baby Sale': Jharkhand Chief Minister Orders Probe* [Video file]. (2018, July 11). Retrieved from https://youtu.be/nsPey2CqYQc?t=658

[120] Mirror Now. Exclusive Breaking News, Twitter [Video file] (2018, July 14,). Retrieved from https://twitter.com/MirrorNow/status/1018046532359032832

Sister Consilia: "Two more."
Police officer: "Where did you sell them?"
Sister Consilia: "Where? I mean, I don't know the addresses."
Police officer: "Who knows them then?"
Sister Consilia: "I need to look at the files."
Police officer: "So, you sold three babies, or were there four?"
Sister Consilia: "We gave one kid away without taking any money."
Police officer: "And?"
Sister Consilia: "That's all."
In separate video that was released, Ms. Indwar was interviewed by a police officer and she also confessed to illegally selling children.[121]
Police officer: "Where do you live?"
Anima Indwar: "Nauasoso, Pura".
Police officer: "Where do you work?".
Anima Indwar: "Missionaries of Charity."
Police officer: "How many kids have you sold?"
Anima Indwar: "Three".
Police officer: "Where?"
Anima Indwar: "Morabadi, Kantatoli."
Police officer: "And Simdega?"
Anima Indwar: "That one we gave away for free."
Police officer: "The one that you sold in UP (Uttar Pradesh), how much did you charge for him?"
Anima Indwar: "One Lakh twenty thousand rupees." ($1700 USD)
Police officer: "Who gave you the money?"
Anima Indwar: "The buyer himself."
Police officer: "Who was the middleman?"
Anima Indwar: "The guard."
Police officer: "Who else was involved?"

---

[121] MirrorNow. Exclusive Breaking News, Twitter [Video file] (July 14, 2019). Retrieved from https://twitter.com/MirrorNow/status/1018046532359032832

Anima Indwar's confession starts at 0.57 seconds.

Anima Indwar: "No one else. Just me, the girl, and the guard."
Police officer: "And she"? (He might be asking about Sister Concilia.)
Anima Indwar: "She was not there."
Police officer: "But she is saying that she was there."
Anima Indwar: "She is saying that, but she was not there."
Police officer: "Did you take her to Missionaries of Charity?"
Anima Indwar: "Yes."

This baby trafficking scandal came to light after Rupa Verma, the chairperson of the Child Welfare Committee in Ranchi, conducted a routine checkup at the shelter, known as Nirmal Hriday. During the checkup, Rupa Verma discovered that there were children missing from the shelter who had been previously registered. Rupa Verma then told the police and an investigation was launched.[122]

Ms. Indwar had been looking after an infant boy and she knew that his biological mother, Karishma Toppo,[123] did not want to keep him. Ms. Indwar then discovered a childless couple from Uttar Pradesh in north India, who was seeking adoption. She offered to sell him for one Lakh twenty thousand rupees ($1,700 USD) and the couple accepted her offer.

When Rupa Verma began asking questions as to why there were children missing at the shelter, Anima Indwar panicked and contacted the couple whom she had previously sold the child to. She then requested that the couple should return to the home to complete certain formalities. When they arrived, Anima Indwar took the infant child away from them. She then returned the boy to Karishma Toppo, his biological mother, without telling the couple who had illegally adopted him.

---

[122] Kumar, H. (July 6, 2018). *Baby Was Sold at Indian Shelter Tied to Mother Teresa, Police Say* - The New York Times.

[123] Brinkmann, S. (2018, July 18). Missionaries of Charity Speak Out on Child Trafficking Charges | Women of Grace. Retrieved from https://www.womenofgrace.com/blog/?p=65229

The couple then complained to the Child Welfare Committee and Rupa Verma confronted Anima Indwar. During the confrontation, Anima Indwar admitted that she had illegally sold four children at the shelter. One child was sold for $750 USD.[124] The police have now rescued all three babies who were sold as well as the one baby who was given away for free by Sister Concilia and Anima Indwar. Anima Indwar and Sister Concilia are both still in jail and Sister Concilia was recently denied bail.[125]

Mother Teresa kept people in destitution at her Missionaries of Charity Homes while accepting millions of dollars from donors, including criminals. Her blind faith led her to cling to Christ for the answer to Bhopal, while she had the most cash-heavy account in the Vatican Bank.[126]

"She had no significant impact on the poor of this city…. She was responsible for creating a negative image of this city. As a Calcuttan I feel totally disgusted by it," said Bikash Ranjan Bhattacharya, who served as mayor of Kolkata from 2005 to 2010.[127]

Meanwhile Mother Teresa, the former "living saint," is now an actual saint—at least in the eyes of the Catholic Church.

To become a saint in the Catholic Church, you need to die first, of course. Then you need to perform two miracles, and the Church has to verify them.[128] This usually takes a long time, starting with a waiting

---

[124] Kumar, H. (July 6, 2018). *Baby Was Sold at Indian Shelter Tied to Mother Teresa, Police Say* - The New York Times.

[125] Indian court denies bail to Missionary of Charity accused of child trafficking. (2019, January 31). Retrieved from https://www.catholicnewsagency.com/news/indian-court-denies-bail-to-missionary-of-charity-accused-of-child-trafficking-78909

[126] 'Cashed-up' *Mother Teresa kept Vatican Bank afloat* – journalist," RT World News

[127] Bengali, S. (2016, September 2). Was Mother Teresa a saint? In city she made synonymous with suffering, a renewed debate over her legacy. Retrieved from https://www.latimes.com/world/la-fg-india-mother-teresa-snap-story.html

[128] Worley, W. (2016, September 3) How do you become a saint? *The Independent*. Retrieved from https://www.independent.co.uk/news/world/europe/how-do-you-become-a-saint-a7224246.html

period of several years after death, but Pope John Paul II allowed Mother Teresa to be fast-tracked.[129]

She died on September 5, 1997; she was beatified, the first official step, on October 19, 2003; less than 20 years after her death, on September 4, 2016, she was canonized as a saint in front of huge crowds at the Vatican.[130]

"This miracle is a hoax."

The first miracle attributed to Mother Teresa, the one that gave justification to her being beatified, was the healing of a tumour in a woman in India.

Monica Besra, from Dangram, India, was suffering from excruciating pain in her abdomen. She could no longer take the agony and decided to leave her family to seek help from the Missionaries of Charity in Calcutta. By coincidence, it was one year after Mother Teresa's death: September 5, 1998. Two sisters, Sister Bartholomea and Sister Ann Sevika, placed a silver locket with Mother's Teresa's picture on top of Besra's stomach where she was experiencing severe pain. According to the story, Besra and the sisters prayed, and later that night she was miraculously healed.[131]

In fact, Besra had been treated at the Balurghat District Hospital in West Bengal before she went to seek help from the Missionaries of Charity Missionaries of Charity. According to hospital records, an ultrasound revealed a tubercular mass (not a cancer) on one of her

---

[129] Compiled By Terence Neilan. (1999, March 2). World Briefing. Retrieved from https://www.nytimes.com/1999/03/02/world/world-briefing.html?module=inline

[130] Perry, J., Hume, T., & Borghese, L. (2016, September 4). Mother Teresa declared a saint by Pope Francis. Retrieved from https://www.cnn.com/2016/09/04/europe/mother-teresa-canonization/index.html

[131] Edamaruku, S. (2017, August 18). Catholic Church manufactured an ovarian miracle for Mother Teresa. Retrieved from https://www.sanaledamaruku.com/single-post/2017/08/18/Catholic-Church-manufactured-an-ovarian-miracle-for-Mother-Teresa

ovaries. After she left the hospital, she continued treatment as an outpatient at the North Bengal Medical College and Hospital until she was released, completely cured in March 1999. A final ultrasound check showed no hint of the tumor. [132]

Dr. Ranjan Mustafi, the chief doctor who treated Besra, says that she was healed with medicine. "It was not a miracle," he said. "She took medicines for nine months to one year."

The Vatican team that went to India to certify the miracle never contacted him. [133]

Besra's husband, Seiku Murmu, said in an interview with *Time* magazine, "My wife did feel less pain one night when she used the locket, but her pain had been coming and going. Then she went to the doctors, and they cured her... My wife was cured by the doctors and not by any miracle...This miracle is a hoax." [134]

Imagine if everyone placed a medallion on top of their injuries and prayed to Mother Teresa, instead of seeking professional medical help. Imagine if there were no hospitals and no one received medical treatment.

What do you think would happen?

Prabir Ghosh is the head of the Science and Rationalist Association of India. Ghosh told *Time* magazine that he will shut down his association and turn over its 2 million rupees ($40,000) to the Catholic Order if the sisters will put the medallion to the test and have it cure another

---

[132] Rubicondior, R. Mother Teresa's Fake Miracle. (2015, March 22). Retrieved from http://rosarubicondior.blogspot.com/2015/03/mother-teresas-fake-miracle.html

[133] Rohde, D. (2003, October 20). Her Legacy: Acceptance And Doubts Of a Miracle. Retrieved from https://www.nytimes.com/2003/10/20/world/her-legacy-acceptance-and-doubts-of-a-miracle.html

[134] Rubicondior, R. Mother Teresa's Fake Miracle. (2015, March 22). Retrieved from http://rosarubicondior.blogspot.com/2015/03/mother-teresas-fake-miracle.html

tumor.[135] But they have not taken up the offer.

Why would Mother Teresa pick Monica Besra, and her alone, to be healed when there are children and families who are suffering throughout the world?

The answer, as I saw it, was that the Church wanted a saint and found an excuse.

Before the Catholic Church could declare Mother Teresa a saint, however, it still needed her to perform a second miracle.

This she is said to have done by curing Marcilio Haddad Andrino, an engineer from Santos, Brazil, of eight abscesses and hydrocephalus (accumulation of cerebrospinal fluid in the brain) in early December 2008.[136]

Why would deceased Mother Teresa step in and select Andrino to be cured of his eight abscesses, and no one else of anything else, when there is so much suffering in the world?

Surely it couldn't have anything to do with the percentage of Catholics in Brazil having fallen from 85 to 63 percent over the past twenty years?[137]

Becoming a saint in the Catholic Church is a costly and time-consuming, process.

> To simply open a cause for beatification costs 50,000 euros, supplemented by the 15,000 euros in actual operating costs. This amount covers the rights of the Holy See and the hefty

---

[135] Rubicondior, R. Mother Teresa's Fake Miracle. (2015, March 22). Retrieved from http://rosarubicondior.blogspot.com/2015/03/mother-teresas-fake-miracle.html

[136] Rubicondior, R. Mother Teresa's Second Miraculous Miracle. (2016, September 3). Retrieved from http://rosarubicondior.blogspot.com/2016/09/mother-teresas-second-miraculous-miracle.htm

[137] Saxena, S. (2016, September 4). In Search of Saint Teresa's Miracle in Brazil. The Wire. Retrieved from https://thewire.in/religion/in-search-of-mother-teresas-miracle-in-brazil

compensation of the expert theologians, physicians, and bishops who examine the cause. After adding the costs of the researchers' time, the drafting of the candidate's positio—a kind of résumé of all his or her works—and finally, the work of the postulator, the amount skyrockets. The average price tag comes to about 500,000 euros. [138]

Meanwhile poor children go without schools, sick people go without hospitals, and millions of people are in desperate need of food and shelter.

Do you think this is the best way to use money, time, and resources?

Perhaps the greatest irony of all is that Mother Teresa had doubts about God's existence. This "saint" who told others to live in faith through their personal connection to God had lost her own sense of connection for long periods of her life.

"Blind faith"

A collection of Mother Teresa's letters to her spiritual advisers and friends titled *Mother Teresa: Come Be My Light* tells us of the darkness within her. An article in *Time* magazine summarizes the truth:

> That absence seems to have started at almost precisely the time she began tending the poor and dying in Calcutta, and—except for a five-week break in 1959—never abated. Although perpetually cheery in public, the Teresa of the letters lived in a state of deep and abiding spiritual pain. In more than 40 communications, many of which have never before been published, she bemoans the "dryness," "darkness," "loneliness" and "torture" she is undergoing. She compares the experience to hell and at one point says it has driven her to

---

[138] Nuzzi, G. (2015). *Merchants in the Temple: Inside Pope Francis's Secret Battle Against Corruption in the Vatican.* New York, England: Henry Holt. p. 33.

doubt the existence of heaven and even of God. [139]

In a 1974 interview, Nodlaig McCarthy asked her, "Now right through history, all the great saints... had great doubts about their faith. They had great moments of absolute darkness when they wondered if there was a God at all. Have you ever had that darkness?" [140]

Mother Teresa responded, "We all have to go through it, yes. That is the time when we have to take greater grip and accept it as a sign of purification of great and greater love. That's the cross, at that time."

In other words, if you cannot feel God, that is a sign that God is working.

McCarthy asked, "When you say we have to take great grip, what exactly do you do when you have a moment of darkness?"

Mother Teresa interrupted: "Cling, cling to Christ because he is the only answer."

McCarthy asked, "And how do you cling to Christ, if you have had along to darkness and you doubt his very existence?"

Mother Teresa replied, "Blind faith."

Blind, yes, and blinding.

McCarthy asked her, "What do you say to people who come to you who say that they have no faith? They admire what you're doing, because naturally their hearts go out to the poor, and the sick and the dying but, they just couldn't do what you're doing, because there is no Christ for them?" [141]

---

[139] Biema, D. V. (2007, August 23). Mother Teresa's Crisis of Faith. Retrieved from http://time.com/4126238/mother-teresas-crisis-of-faith

[140] *Mother Teresa of Calcutta on Irish Television, 1974*. Retrieved from https://youtu.be/Th2QzJwy8tI?t=1394

[141] *Mother Teresa of Calcutta on Irish Television, 1974*. Retrieved from https://youtu.be/Th2QzJwy8tI?t=1445

Mother Teresa responded, "I don't believe that there is any human being who doesn't believe in God, unless they are mental."

I could hardly believe my ears.

This was a final confirmation that Christianity is blind faith.

Mother Teresa, who said that her beliefs were based on nothing other than blind faith, and that if you did not feel God you should take it as a sign of God, was now questioned the mental health of anyone who does not believe in God.

What if you questioned the Church? Where did these thoughts come from?

You have probably already guessed her answer to this. Mother Teresa wrote multiple letters to Sister Margaret Mary, M.C., warning her of the Devil and its ability to interfere with her thoughts:

> Love Jesus & keep a smiling heart for Him. — All these disturbing thoughts come from the devil—ignore them all. God bless you my child. [142]

I found myself back at the beginning of my life, back in Sunday school, where independent thought was blamed on Satan, and fear of the Devil was preached to me.

Mother Teresa preached poverty and was obsessed with human suffering, except when it came to herself. She was taught suffering was the way to become close to Jesus. She lost her father in childhood, and in adulthood took the absence of her feeling of God the Father as proof of his guidance and challenge to her.

As Christopher Hitchens said,

> [Mother Teresa] was not a friend of the poor. She was a friend of poverty. She said that suffering was a gift from God. She

---

[142] Teresa, M., & Kolodiejchuk, B. (2007). *Mother Teresa: Come Be My Light: The Private Writings of the Saint of Calcutta*. Doubleday Religion. Mother Teresa wrote to Sister Margaret Mary, M.C., January 15, 1955. p. 157.

spent her life opposing the only known cure for poverty, which is the empowerment of women and the emancipation of them from a livestock version of compulsory reproduction. [143]

I had not found a saint in Mother Teresa. I had found someone who helped create and maintain a hell on earth, all in the service of keeping people subjugated to the cruel absent God she worshiped and the institution that sold this illusion to control people.

She spent her whole life in a bubble of fear and delusion. She didn't try to escape it. She worked to bring and keep others into it.

---

[143] Hitchens, C. (2003, October 20). The Fanatic, Fraudulent Mother Teresa. Retrieved from https://slate.com/news-and-politics/2003/10/the-fanatic-fraudulent-mother-teresa.html

NO ONE IS SPECIALLY CHOSEN

Throughout my life, as a Christian, I believed that I was special, until my good friends Tim and Jason Keck asked me, "What makes you so special?"

The belief that I was special had been planted in my mind since Sunday school. When they asked me this question, I gave it much deeper thought, and realized that there was nothing special about me except for incredibly good luck.

I then came up with an invisible belief system that Christians live in inside of their bubble and I called it "special agreements."

Christians have special agreements with Jesus, God, their religion, or their own mind. They believe that they are specially chosen, and the universe is looking out for them. They think that they can commit sin and then go to church and pray and be forgiven by God and Jesus, and it is all based on fear, superstition, and blind faith.

I looked the other way when I saw orphan children living outside of majestic churches in the Philippines. I also looked away when I saw dogs chained on rooftops surrounded by barbed wire fences, in direct sunlight in tropical temperatures.

This was an example of my own special agreement with Christianity. I feared the Church and believed that injustices did not apply to me because I believed in Jesus Christ as the Lord and Savior.

If God is giving humans dominion over all other creatures and dominion is to be accepted as: "must be understood in terms of caregiving, even nurturing, not exploitation,"[144] why is the Lord God appeased by animal sacrifice? Why does He love the smell of their flesh burning?

Why would a loving God create vulnerable beings and allow them to be exploited, raped, tortured, mutilated, and killed by humans, when it is completely unnecessary? I challenge you to watch Dominion,[145] a documentary which reveals the truth of what is happening to trillions of vulnerable, non-human animals, in the animal agriculture industry, each year.

Is it logical to believe that a loving God would only look out for certain individuals, but not for people who never had the opportunity to learn about Christianity, or the trillions of other non-human animals who also never had the opportunity to believe?

Christians are not special. I'm not special. No one is special.

In Peter Buffett's great book, *Life is What You Make It: Find Your Own Path to Fulfillment*, he shares some great wisdom:

> No one gets to choose his parents or to have a say in the circumstances of her birth. A life may begin in a snug and comfortable bedroom in an American suburb or on a straw mat in a mud hut in West Africa. The parents could be residents of a Park Avenue penthouse, or homeless people barely surviving in a public park. They might be healthy, or they might be infected with HIV. They could be athletes and scholars, or crack addicts and criminals. They could be partners in a committed couple for whom parenthood will be one of life's high points, or they could be virtual strangers out

---

[144] R. Pregeant, *For the Healing of the Nation: A Biblical Vision*.

[145] Monson, S. (Producer), Delforce, C., (Director) & Jayne., L. (Assistant Director). (2018). *Dominion* [Documentary]. Australia: Aussie Farms. Retrieved from https://www.dominionmovement.com/watch

on a date, completely indifferent to the consequences of their actions.[146]

From Buffett I realized I could have been born as anything under the sun, at any point in history. Buffett increased my compassion and understanding that life is wonderful—a true miracle, not a fraud—and I must do my best to make the world a better place.

---

[146] Buffett, P. (2010). *Life Is What You Make It*. New York: Three Rivers Press. p. 27.

A STRICT RELATIONSHIP

People stay conditioned by the Christian faith for two primary reasons:
1. The belief that they will go to Heaven when they die.
2. The fear of going to Hell and spending eternity with the Devil for not believing.

Christianity tells people that they were specially chosen. And at the same time, it tells them that they are sinful, bad people, who are only being saved from eternal punishment by strict obedience. This is a classic abusive relationship.

The only thing we truly have to fear is fear itself.

Christians fear being punished by their God for not attending Church. They become defensive and offended when challenged about their God and their religion. Lots of Christians, including the man who I approached wearing the CG jacket, have special agreements. They believe that God put the world here for them to enjoy, and is looking out for them, but not for non-Christians or others who never had the opportunity to believe.

Christians having special agreements is not their fault because they were conditioned to think this way, as I was in Sunday School. Growing up, because of my religious beliefs, I was certain that people would go to Hell for not believing. That meant Muslims, Buddhists, Jewish people, and anyone else who was not Christian: all doomed to spending eternity in Hell with the Devil.

The Bible preaches superstition, tyranny, sexism, slavery, violence, animal sacrifice, homophobia, and prejudice. It is based on blind faith and promotes irrational thought and creates separation in society between people.

Burst the bubble. Burst the Bible—and replace it with love, gratitude, and compassion.

BURSTING THE BUBBLE

The bubble I had been living inside of burst after spending three years of my life living in the Philippines. I made the connection that I had grown up with unbelievable privilege and opportunity. It had never occurred to me that it is an absolute miracle to have the opportunity to eat three meals in a day, until I saw orphan children starving in the Philippines.

There are many small things we can do that give love and light to others. In 2014, I had fourteen tickets for Derek Jeter's final game at Camden Yards in Baltimore that I was originally planning on selling. Then I started to think about how grateful I am to be alive, and then I thought it would be awesome to give these tickets to orphan children who never had the opportunity to go to baseball games. I wanted them to have the opportunity to see Derek Jeter play one final time.

So, I donated the tickets to The Children's Home in Baltimore, and I got an overwhelming feeling of gratitude that forever changed my life.

This was first time that I experienced joy to the fullest. I could not sleep for several days because I was filled up with so much energy, joy, and happiness.

Since this experience, I became a human and animal rights activist and co-founded The Light Movement with my great friend Chris McGinn.

McGinn is a great person who has influenced millions of people with his relentless online activism. He educates people on human rights issues as well as the horrific injustice of the animal agriculture industry.

The Light Movement has held marches for human and animal liberation in Toronto, Boston, Utah, and Las Vegas.

WHAT SHOULD I BELIEVE? WHAT SHOULD I DO?

Should I fear death? Should I fear Hell and the Devil? Thomas Paine was asked the same question. He answered:

> I find that death has no terrors for me. As to the people called Christians, they have no evidence that their religion is true. There is no more proof that the Bible is the Word of God, than that the Koran of Mahomet is the Word of God. It is education makes all the difference. Man, before he begins to think for himself, is as much the child of habits in Creeds as he is in plowing and sowing. Yet creeds, like opinions, prove nothing. [147]

During Thomas Paine's last moments of life, two Presbyterian ministers forced their way past his housekeeper and pressured him to accept Jesus Christ. They asked him, "Do you wish to believe that Jesus Christ is the son of God?" Paine responded: "I have no wish to believe on that subject." [148]

I believe in what Robert Ingersoll said that: "Every mind should be true to itself—should think, investigate and conclude for itself." When I wake up each day, I know life is a miracle and I must do my best to make the most of it.

---

[147] Paine, T. & Fonder, P.S. (1969). *The Complete Writings of Thomas Paine*, vol. II. New York: The Citadel Press. pp. 1483–1485. Retrieved from http://www.stephenjaygould.org/ctrl/paine_lad.html

[148] Hitchens, C. (2006). *Thomas Paine's Rights of Man.* New York, NY: Grove/Atlantic. p. 140.

What, then, can make me a good person? What is the point of life?

We gather meaning by helping others, which gives us purpose and fulfillment while striving to make the world a better place.

We can become activists.

We live in a world where over 60 billion land animals and 2.7 trillion marine aquatic animals are needlessly being tortured, killed, and mutilated for food.[149] We can go vegan.

We are living in a world where nearly a billion people are either starving or go to bed hungry each night.[150]

We can help woman by campaigning for woman's rights.

Homeless people also need our help.

Life's meaning is not hidden inside a book written thousands of years ago. We do not create meaning and happiness with blind faith.

We create it with our own actions. An ounce of action trumps a ton of theory.

I have learned to focus on gratitude while living in the present moment. There are so many things to be grateful for: Friends, family, relationships, love, health, and technology. Having the ability to see, hear, taste, smell, and touch are all little miracles.

We have been given the miracle of life. We are in heaven right now. It is up to us to make our own wings.

Let's do our best to make the world the best place it can possibly be. A world of equality and caring for every being we share this world with, the only world we know. A world where the only bubbles are the vegan soap bubbles, we blow that are filled with love, gratitude,

---

[149] Factory Farms - A Well-Fed World. (n.d.). Retrieved from http://awfw.org/factory-farms

[150] Food Aid Foundation. World Hunger Statistics. (n.d.). Retrieved from https://www.foodaidfoundation.org/world-hunger-statistics.html

compassion, and happiness, as we watch them flowing through the air, soaring into the light.

ACKNOWLEDGMENTS

I am grateful for the miracle of life and I am incredibly grateful that I was born in Canada. Being born as a Canadian gave me the freedom and opportunity to travel the world, which opened my mind and gave me perspective.

Thank you to my parents, Scott and Karen, for allowing me to pursue my dreams in life. I am grateful to my uncle, Dave Barker, for helping me write the introduction to this book and helping to improve the cover.

Thank you, Derek Young, for being an amazing friend and giving me a Kindle, which led me to read and write relentlessly. Thank you for helping me write the back-cover blurb as well as the subtitle.

Thank you, Tim Keck, for being a great friend and providing wisdom and encouragement for me to write this book.

Thank you, Erin Janus, your awesome YouTube video on fulfillment inspired me to focus 100% on writing and completing this book.

Thank you, Chris McGinn, for being a great friend and thank you for your indefatigable, utterly relentless dedication to human and animal rights activism on the Light Movement.

Thank you, James Harbeck, for being a great editor. You did a great job of giving this book structure and flow.

Thank you, Les, for doing a great job on the cover design for The Christian Bubble.

Thank you, Ruth Chernia, for doing a good job of editing the second pass, and thank you to Laura Wilkinson for doing a good job of editing as well.

Thank you, Marc. J. Seifer, for dedicating seventeen years of your life to writing *Wizard: The Life and Times of Nikola Tesla Biography of a Genius*. Your wonderful book changed my life forever.

Thank you, Dr. Aroup Chatterjee, for your relentless determination and perseverance uncovering the truth about Mother Teresa. Your great book, *Mother Teresa The Untold Story,* opened my mind to the truth about Mother Teresa and it increased my compassion and ability to handle obstacles. I am forever grateful for your hard work and dedication.

Thank you to the late, and great, Christopher Hitchens for your relentless work uncovering the truth about Mother Teresa and her Missionaries of Charity.

Thank you, Shobhan Saxena, for writing your great article 'In Search of Saint Teresa's Miracle in Brazil.' Also, thank you for talking to me on Twitter, I really appreciate it.

Thank you to Rosa Rubicondior, Sanal Edamaruku, and Jaideep Mazumdar for exposing the truth about how the Catholic Church manufactured miracles 10 years after Mother Teresa's death to make Mother Teresa a saint.

Thank you, Hari Kumar, for reporting and writing about The Missionaries of Charities trafficking children. Also, thank you Hari, for responding to me on Twitter, and thank you for responding to my email, I really appreciate it.

Thank you, Vishal Palve, for translating Sister Consilia's and Anima Indwar's confession to illegally selling children from Hindi to English, I am super grateful.

Thank you, to Susan Shields for writing your great article 'House of

Illusions' which exposed the truth about Mother Teresa's congregation, the Missionaries of Charity. Thank you, Julia Lavarnway, and thank you to The Center for Inquiry, for granting me permission to use Susan Shields great article in this book.

Thank you, Penn Jillette and Teller, and your entire team for your wonderful documentary "Penn & Teller: Bullshit!" Holier Than Thou. Your TV show enlightened me with the truth about Mother Teresa and her Missionaries of Charities Organization.

Thank you, Peter Buffett, for helping me find my path to fulfillment and opening my mind with your wonderful book: *Life is What You Make it: Find Your Own Path to Fulfillment.*

Thank you, Calvin Ayre and Anita Krajnc, for being tremendous leaders and influencing me to take action and become a human and animal rights activist.

Thank you, Mark Cuban, for teaching me that time is the most precious asset and you should be doing what is most important with time. Your life lesson made me realize that it was an absolute must to complete this book.

Thank you, Kevin O'Leary, for writing *Cold Hard Truth on Business and Money,* and thank you for influencing me to tell people the cold hard truth.

Thank you, Sir Richard Branson, for writing *Like a Virgin,* and thank you for influencing me to try LSD.

Thank you, Albert Hofman, for discovering LSD. Your wonderful discovery, taken in extremely small dosages, helped me to open my mind while living in the present moment.

Thank you, Lauri Grenier, for writing *Invent It, Sell It, Bank It!,* your great book taught me about taking risks while focusing on gratitude.

Thank you, Robert Herchavek, for teaching me to work hard and never complain!

Thank you, Tai Lopez, for teaching me the importance of reading every day.

Thank you, Tim Ferriss, for your podcasts and thank you for writing great books and for teaching me about the 80/20 principles.

Thank you, Dave Asprey, for your wonderful podcasts which helped me think and learn at an accelerated pace.

Thank you, Nikola Tesla and Swami Vivekananda, for teaching me to do my best to make the world a better place each and every day.

Thank you, Mihaly Csikszentmihalyi and Steven Kotler, for teaching me about the flow state of mind with your great books: *Flow* and *The Rise of Superman*.

Thank you, Charlie Munger, Dan Rather, and James Patterson, for teaching me the importance of rewriting, which helped me strengthen this book.

Thank you, Jeff Bezos, for creating Amazon Kindle, and thank you for providing the opportunity to publish this book on your website.

Thank you, Charlie Tian, for giving me the chance to write for GuruFocus, which gave me the opportunity to practice writing.

Thank you to the late, and great, Thomas Paine, for being a relentless human and animal rights activist.

Thank you to all the motivational speakers and people who I have had the opportunity to listen to and keep me motivated as I faced adversity and hurdled obstacle after obstacle. Tim Grover, Daymond John, Grant Cardone, Larry Ellison, Elon Musk, Ryan Holiday, Barbara Corcoran, Jerry Jones, and Jennifer Lopez. I am forever grateful for your wisdom and leadership.

Thank you, Tom Karadza, for teaching me about building and maintaining momentum in life.

Thank you so much, Frank Ungaro, for founding Brasa Niagara

Brazilian Jiu Jitsu. You taught me self-discipline which increased my confidence and ability to accomplish this book.

Thank you so much to Project Share for providing me with food which gave me the energy that I needed to complete this book. I am super incredibly grateful.

Thank you, Mary, for allowing me to live and rent a room at your house for six months while I completed this book.

Thank you, Lee Manning, for being a good friend and thank you for reminding me that I needed to finish this book in a timely manner.

Thank you to all the human and animal rights activists throughout the world for making the world a better place.

I love you all!

Made in the USA
Columbia, SC
14 March 2019